The Owl and The Horseshoe

By Debra Hughey

Wake Forest, NC

www.scuppernongpress.com

The Owl and The Horseshoe

©2015 Debra Hughey

First Printing

The Scuppernong Press
PO Box 1724
Wake Forest, NC 27588
www.scuppernongpress.com

Cover and book design by Frank B. Powell, III

All rights reserved. Printed in the United States of America.

No part of this book may be reproduced or transmitted in any form or by any means, electronic or mechanical, including photocopying, recording, or by any information and storage and retrieval system, without written permission from the editor and/or publisher.

International Standard Book Number ISBN 978-1-942806-01-1

Library of Congress Control Number: 2015939287

Table of Contents

Foreword 1

Part One —
  Hillabee Town near the Tallapoosa, Time of the New
  Leaves, 1796 3

Part Two —
  Hillabee Town, Time of the New Leaves, 1802 37

Part Three —
  Hillabee Town, Time of the Falling Leaves, 1811 71

Part Four —
  Tohopeka, Time of the New Leaves, 1814 149

Epilogue 175

Glossary of Creek Words 177

Acknowledgements 179

Photos 180

Maps 183

Foreword

The little girl's scream was barely heard over the musket and cannon fire coming from the hillside. The closer sound of the prophet's chant and the warrior's yell almost drowned out her cry of terror. She had been told by her mother and grandmother not to go near the river, to stay close to the huti with the other children.

The women knew they were there, the white men with the horses, the Cherokee from the north and the Creek from the lower towns, those who had taken the way of the hated whites. The women realized the danger and feared for the children, they knew no route of escape existed … where would they go?

After crossing the river in the canoes taken from the east bank by the Cherokee braves, the warriors, both white and red infiltrated the village. The little girl screamed again as she was knocked to the ground by the rushing men. Strong brown arms pulled her from the ground and carried the frightened girl to a place of safety behind a clump of bushes. The young Creek warrior, looking no different from the warriors of her own town, made the sign for silence as he quickly moved away, the white feather in his hair bobbing up and down.

The day of the child's scream would be written about by historians and writers of books as the big battle on the Tallapoosa. This day, for the little girl and her people, was one of great sadness and loss. A loss not only felt then, but for hundreds of years in the future. The day the power of the Creek Nation was broken, Sunday, the twenty-seventh day of March in the year 1814. The day of the Battle of Tohopeka, the battle at the horseshoe, or as the white militia called it, the Battle of Horseshoe Bend.

This is a story leading up to that event and of what would happen to the Creek people who lived and experienced that sad episode of their history. Historical facts are accurate, at least as accurate as white historians would write them, and many of the characters were real. Menawa, Monahee and Red Eagle certainly lived and the strong, overpowering but self glorifying Andrew Jackson left his mark on time and generations of native people.

The family characters are fictitious. The story provides a normal element of how the native people of the time lived, played, loved and died ... and of how they faced the day of the Horseshoe.

Part One
Hillabee Town on the Tallapoosa
Time of the New Leaves, 1796

Chapter One

As first light edged over the eastern horizon, the muddy water of White Oak Creek began spilling over its bank, making walking near the stream treacherous. The storm from the previous night had left evidence of its wrath, breaking limbs from the hickory and oaks and uprooting several small dogwoods. The Hillabee people realized they had been fortunate; the Great Spirit had protected them from any real danger to their town. None had been injured, all the huti were still standing. The tree limbs could be used for firewood. The people would make the best of the situation.

Cleanup of the Hillabee mother town, ideally located at the confluence of the White Oak and Little Hillabee Creek, began before the morning meal was prepared. Each person in the town had responsibilities, even the older children.

Sunflower Woman watched the rapid flow of White Oak Creek continue to rise. Much rain must have fallen up Oakfuskee River and the other streams for the normally small creek to be so great now.

"Little Flower." Having to call loudly to be heard over the rushing stream, Sunflower Woman again called out to her only daughter. "Little Flower, use much caution. Do not go near the stream, you and the other girls can pick up the limbs on the other side of the huti."

Thirteen year old Little Flower and her friends had never seen the small stream overflow to this extent. While they were somewhat frightened there was also a bit of excitement as they ran back and forth, each with an arm full of tree limbs. Little Flower's older brother and his companion, Young Eagle, had heard his mother's warning to his sister. They realized the danger too, but were not close enough to prevent Little Flower from slipping into the rushing, muddy stream.

"Little Flower!" Brown Hawk yelled as he and Young Eagle ran toward the creek. Young Eagle quickly jumped in as Little Flower was swept down stream, her black hair trailing behind her. Being a strong swimmer, as were all young Creek braves, and allowing the current to carry him, Young Eagle managed to reach the little girl only seconds before a log protruding from the water surely would have caused serious injury. Quickly picking up a large limb from one of the fallen trees, Brown Hawk ran beside the creek and was there to extend the life-saving limb to his friend, who then grabbed the end and pulled himself and Little Flower to safety.

Young Eagle and Little Flower lay on the muddy bank both gasping for breath as the townspeople gathered around them. "Oh, my Little Flower," Sunflower Woman screamed as the crowd parted to let the fearful mother through. "My child, are you alright? You should not have gotten so near the stream." Seeing that her child was indeed unhurt, Sunflower Woman turned her attention to the young brave who had an ugly gash on his leg. "Thank you Young Eagle, you have saved the life of my child and for that you will be forever in my favor. I see you have been injured."

Fifteen year-old Young Eagle, who eagerly looked forward to receiving his warrior name, was well-liked in the town. Everyone believed that he would be a brave warrior in the future. He slowly pulled himself from the muddy creek bank. "My mother," he said, addressing Sunflower Woman in the traditional way young men spoke to all women. "Your child was in danger. I only did what was necessary and I know that others would have done the same." Young Eagle turned and extended his hand to help Little Flower to stand. "Little one, you really should be more careful." And with a slight smile he said, "I will always be around to help you."

Little Flower, embarrassed at the scene she had caused, quickly stood. "Thank you Young Eagle. I am sorry I was not careful. In the future I will be. Come now to our huti so that my mother can see to your injury."

"It is not so bad Little Flower, Brown Hawk and I need to help the others with the cleanup. You go and see if the grandmothers are preparing the morning meal." Again with a smile, "Swimming has made my appetite big."

The Hillabee people all returned to their duties again, thanking the Great Spirit for sparing the lives of the two young people. Later in the day, after the stream had returned to normal and the village had been cleaned from the storm, the Hinibas, the man responsible for planning celebrations, decided today was a good day to celebrate.

The town crier had gone throughout the village, calling for all women to bring their pots of dried corn and beans and for the hunters to bring fresh venison and turkey and for the children to bring hickory nuts left from the season of falling leaves. Everyone was expected to come. Runners had been sent out the adjoining paths to the four smaller Hillabee towns.

Members from the Raccoon, the Potato, the Turkey, the Bear, Wolf, Bird, and Deer, and of course Wind clans would all attend. Trader Grierson and his Indian family certainly would come and the Hillabee Micco had heard from a runner that Oakfuskee town warrior, Hothlepoya, was in the area, and he too would be at the celebration.

Chapter Two

The warm rays from the midday sun filtered down through the new leaves of the hardwood trees, as people from all of the Hillabee towns converged around the square ground. The morning had been long, one filled with anxiety and later much difficult work.

Now, spirits were high. Groups of warriors talked quietly about rumors of more white encroachments and treaties not honored by the white father in Washington. The women shared the latest gossip and the children ran and played in total abandon, forgetting about the near tragedy earlier in the day.

The group of men and women parted, calling the children to their side, each settling into the assigned places, as Gray Fox, the Hinihas followed by the Hillabee Micco, entered the square ground.

The chatter and laughter diminished to a low mummer of anticipation as Gray Fox stepped into view, all eagerly awaiting the upcoming words. The sharp rap of a single drum beat signaled silence, even the youngest child understanding.

"Welcome people of all Hillabee Towns." Gray Fox said, turning slowly in all directions to encompass everyone in the square ground. "Listen now to the great Hillabee Micco."

As was the custom in all Creek towns, any celebration or ceremony began with speeches, some very lengthy, from the Miccos and beloved men of the town. While everyone, especially the warriors, were very interested in what the town leaders had to say, it was hoped that on this day, the speeches would be short. As if understanding the desire of his people, the Hillabee Micco began by saying, "I wish to welcome each of you to the mother town of the Hillabee. I wish to extend a special welcome to our esteemed leader, Crazy Trouble Hunter, who has journeyed up river from Oakfuskee Town to meet with us on this day. The Great Spirit has shown good favor in sparing our town once again from the wrath of the storm of new leaves. More importantly, the Great Spirit gave much courage to one of our young warriors." Neither Young Eagle nor Little Flower had expected any mention of the morning's near tragedy. Little Flower could fill the rosy flush cover her brown face. With dignity uncommon in one so inexperienced, Young Eagle lifted his shoulders and looked directly at the Micco, not showing the emotion that raced through his heart.

"The rains caused our little stream to fill over the banks and any of our people could have become a victim of the raging water. While attempting to fulfill her responsibility to our town, the daughter of Sunflower Woman tread too close and the ground gave way beneath the child, sweeping her into the stream. This meeting today could have been one of mourning were it not for the quick actions of Young Eagle and the brother of Little Flower. Young Eagle jumped into the water and swam to Little Flower while Brown Hawk extended a long limb to Young Eagle, pulling them to safety. Both of the young warriors will receive their name of honor at the time of Poskeeta. On this day we will celebrate the lives of our youth and of the coming of the warm season. We will ask the Great Spirit to provide us with ample harvest to provide our food and also for the good health of the Hillabee people." The Hillabee Chief paused as the shrill cry of a red tail hawk could be heard as it circled overhead. This was taken as a good omen and brown faces smiled as the village people searched the sky for the large raptor. "I will end my talk now. I ask for the vaunted military leader of the people of the upper Oakfuskee to speak."

The quiet murmurs that occurred as the hawk continued to circle over the village ceased as Hothlepoya, known as Crazy Trouble Hunter, stood before the crowd. It was very rare indeed for one of such importance to appear before a general crowd which included women and children. His presence was usually reserved for council with head men and the warriors. Born in 1765, in his town of Oakfuskee, Crazy Trouble Hunter was young to have achieved such status. Only a few years would pass before he would become more important and renowned. The military leader who stood before the Hillabee people this day would be known as Menawa. Many in the future would talk of his courage to live and to die. Some said he was not of full blood, that his father was Scotch or English. A few even thought he was not Creek at all but was Shawnee. His linage was of very little consequence as he was judged by his great prowess in battle, his leadership ability and the kindness of heart he showed for his people. This kindness would shine even now as he slowly began to talk. "People of the Hillabee, it is with great pleasure that I come before you today. I am honored to share this great time of celebration. I too thank the Great Spirit, the Giver of Breath, for sparing not only this town but all of the towns of the Hillabee and the Oakfuskee. I am joyful in my heart that the lives of two of the young people were spared. May both see the season of new leaves many times and continue living their lives in the way of the Hillabee people. My words will not be of great length as today is one of celebration. Let us now all celebrate."

Surprised at the short duration of the speech, neither which were actually speeches at all; the town people left the square, each doing their part in preparing for the upcoming festivities. Only a few had understood the underlying meaning of what Hothlepoya had said regarding the future. While everyone enjoyed the addition of the new items, the iron hatchet, the kettle and the trinkets that the white traders, including Mr. Grierson, had brought into their lives, some of the older ones realized the danger, the danger that the way of the Hillabee people would not remain the same. They also could sense the very real danger of more intrusion from the very people who had made their lives easier, the white man.

These troubling thoughts were soon forgotten as excitement filled the air, still smelling of freshly broken tree limbs. This would be the first celebration of any kind in many moons and everyone was eager to begin.

Chapter Three

Little Flower, still embarrassed from the commotion she had caused earlier, was busy helping her mother carry their food contribution to the area prepared for the feast. Her father, brother of the Hillabee King, had killed a large buck the day before and the freshly dressed deer had been roasted only hours ago. The fragrant aroma of the still warm meat made her mouth water and she could hardly wait to taste the bread made from dried corn.

"Little Flower, please return to our huti and get the basket of hickory nuts," Sunflower Woman said as she took the bread from her daughter. "And put on the new moccasins we just made for you. I think on this day you too shall dance in the ribbon dance with the women and older girls."

"My mother, do you mean that I can dance with you?" Little Flower asked, trying hard to hide her excitement. She had never been allowed to do this before and was surprised that her mother would permit her to dance now.

"Yes, my daughter today will be your first. This, after all, is a day of celebration and we are celebrating not only this day but the many days and seasons ahead for you, Young Eagle, your brother Brown Hawk and all the other Hillabee young people. Sunflower Woman tucked a strand of her daughter's black hair back into place. "It has been brought to my attention today that you soon will be a woman. In only two moons, in the time of the red berries, you will enter your fourteenth season and you have learned already the many responsibilities of the Hillabee woman. I think today you will dance."

"This is good, my mother, I will return with the nuts and my moccasins," Little Flower said as she warmly embraced her mother. "And I will not fall into the waters of White Oak Creek this time. Mother, I say now how sorry I am to have created such a scene this morning. That was not the action of a woman."

"Little Flower, that was an accident. You did not fall in.

The ground beneath your feet gave way. Anyone walking there would have been pulled into the water. Your action was one of courage, not fear, as you stayed afloat until Young Eagle could get to you. Many have told me this. You may have gone into the water a child, but in coming out, you became a young woman. Now, go quickly to our huti, the others are ready to begin."

The moon of new leaves was not a time of bountiful food for the Hillabee people. Still too early for planting and the berries that would be plentiful in a few weeks were only now showing their tiny green leaves. This meant the women needed to be resourceful in preparing food for the celebration. Venison, turkey and fish had been prepared along with kettles and pots of stews made from rabbits and turtles mixed with dried corn and beans. Many, including Sunflower Woman, had prepared bread made from ground corn. The routine bowls of sofkee had been laced with early season honey to make the dish tasty. Trader Grierson had bought from the trading post favorites for the children and women and also a few bottles of rum which he would sparingly divide among the men. Too much of the white man's fire water would not be tolerated.

After the meal had been finished and all of the Hillabee people proclaimed to be totally satisfied with the food which had been quickly prepared, the Miccos and warriors entered the council house. This was the time for the pipe to be passed and for the men to drink accee, the black drink. The opportunity could not be passed by for some serious talk among the beloved men and war leaders. The men were all eager to hear the words Hothlepoya would say in the absence of the women.

"My brothers," he began as he accepted the pipe from the Hillabee King, "there is now an uneasy feeling throughout the nation of the Muscogee. The Great White Fathers talk with a forked tongue, making promises they do not intend to honor." Murmurs of agreement coursed throughout the council house. "They take the land and say they need no more…that they want to live in peace with their red brethren, then in only a few suns they want to treat with us again and more land is asked for." Pausing briefly, the famed leader looked over the crowd of warriors and leaders. "I say we watch and we listen with much caution and we allow the white race no more of the land that belongs to the red people."

The tone of the leader's voice implied the seriousness of his statement. No one in the council house uttered a word, the eyes of each warrior still fixed on Hothlepoya. "Some have said we will fight. I say now is not the time. We must prepare and unite as a people. When the time is right…we will be ready."

Remaining quiet no longer, the warriors, seemingly all in unison, began the ancient war cry given by their race from time immortal. Pleased with the response, Hothlepoya continued, "I will talk no more on war and the white people who choose to force us to fight. Today we will celebrate. Now let us partake of the accee and allow the women to dance."

Chapter Four

The women seated in the square ground near the council house, while not hearing the words of Hothlepoya, did hear the war cries of the warriors and they realized the importance of the talk. They also realized their men were in a festive mood now and the dancing and merry making would last long into the night.

"My mother," Little Flower said as she secured the ribbons of many colors onto her belt, "my stomach feels as if it is filled with many butterflies fluttering all around. I must have had too much of the flavored sofkee and bread made of corn."

Sunflower Woman laughed at her daughter as she untangled a ribbon on her belt. "Oh! I do not think so; you are only a little bit nervous. I know you will dance well. Have you not practiced many times?"

"Yes mother, but no one else looked at me when I was dancing then and they will now because this is the first time and all of our people will know this."

The drums signaled the first dance would begin soon and all the women and young maidens began walking toward the center of the square ground. Their dance would be the first of many.

Taking Little Flower's hand, Sunflower Woman stepped into the circle. "Are you ready, my child," She asked as the soft beat of the drum began slowly escalating to a faster rhythm.

"Yes, my mother, I am ready." Forgetting the butterflies in her stomach, Little Flower joined with the women and other girls, some like her, dancing for the first time in the square ground.

"Look, Young Eagle," Brown Hawk said as he and his companion joined the other young men and warriors at the square ground. "I see Little Flower. I did not know she would dance on this day. I think she is still a child and not old enough to dance with the women, but she does look a little pretty and not at all like the drenched little girl from this morning."

"My friend, you only have the eyes of a brother when you look at Little Flower," Young Eagle answered as he watched her dance in perfect unison with the women, her colorful ribbons flying around her tiny waist. "Your little sister will one day be a beautiful woman and many warriors will seek her favor. See how graceful she dances and …"

"Young Eagle, are you serious? That is Little Flower you are speaking of. She is my sister. How can you say this?" Brown Hawk asked his friend in disbelief as he looked from the circle of dancing women to Young Eagle.

"She is the sister of Brown Hawk not Young Eagle and …" feeling a little bit embarrassed Young Eagle quickly added, "I am talking about the future, not now you silly Hawk, now let us go. I think there is a game of chunkee to be played."

Both young men rose to leave the square ground. As he was leaving, Young Eagle glanced once more at the circle of dancing women and his eyes locked with those of Little Flower. For only a few seconds the stomach of Young Eagle quivered like butterflies. "I must have had too much bread made from the corn," he said to himself as Little Flower danced by.

After what seemed like only a short time to Little Flower, the first dance of the day was over and others began to enter the dance circle. She breathlessly sat down next to her mother to watch the dancing. "Oh, my mother, that was such fun. Will I be allowed to dance again today?"

"Of course you may Little Flower," Sunflower Woman said, answering her daughter. "And you did very well. I am very proud and so is your father. For now you should rest and watch. To watch is to learn and the time is near for you to learn many new things."

Chapter Five

The dancing and merry making did last long into the night. Little Flower and the young maidens were allowed to participate in several more dances before the dance for the young women and warriors of courting age began. Little Flower and her friends had watched this dance before, but this time she was more attentive and realized that soon she too would dance with the young warriors.

Little Flower seemed mesmerized as she continued to watch the young couples dance, their bodies at once touching and then pulling away, always in rhythm with the beat of the drum.

"I can hardly wait until you and I can dance this dance and I know which of the young warriors I want to be my partner and I also know which one you will choose." The familiar voice of Little Flower's best friend, Spotted Fawn, made her jump. "Oh Spotted Fawn, has this not been the most exciting day? Are we not too young to think about dancing with a warrior and…" Little Flower paused not sure how to express her confusing thoughts, "and be touched by him?"

"We are not that young. See, my sister is dancing and she is only one summer older than us. Do you not want to know which warrior I would dance with and the one I think will dance with you?" Spotted Fawn asked with her brown eyes dancing like the firelight. "Yes," said Little Flower, "please tell me. We have no secrets. But how can you know who I would dance with when I do not know?"

"You do know. It may be that you do not realize it but you know. First I will tell you about the one I would choose." Spotted Fawn edged a little closer to Little Flower before revealing her secret. "I will dance with the one who will make us sisters and not just friends. I will dance with the brother of Little Flower. I will dance with Brown Hawk."

"Brown Hawk," Little Flower said, almost too loudly. Brown Hawk, that mischievous …" Before she could finish calling her brother any names, Spotted Fawn quickly, still trying to speak softly, said, "yes, Brown Hawk is spirited and he will one day soon make a fine, brave warrior and he has strong arms that I would…" suddenly Spotted Fawn paused, embarrassed by her own thoughts, "arms that I would love for him to hold me with. So there, now you know that I do not look at Brown Hawk as a brother as do you."

"My Friend, why have you not spoken of this before and how long have you had these kinds of feelings for my brother? And I still want to know who it is that I would dance?"

"I think for many suns, but I just realized today, that special feeling. One that is more than just for the brother of my friend, and as for you …" Spotted Fawn stopped speaking as two young warriors appeared from the shadows beyond the square ground. "There is your answer."

Brown Hawk and Young Eagle walked toward the girls as the final beat from the drums diminished. "Little Flower," Brown Hawk called out. "Our mother would like for you to come sit by her side for the final dance of the night and Spotted Fawn, your mother too would like for you to come."

The girls looked at each other and smiled, one with an "I told you so" look and the other with a look of agreement. "Yes, my brother, we will come. Where will you and Young Eagle go?" Little Flower asked, almost afraid to steal a glance at Young Eagle. "My sister, we will dance the dance of the warriors this night, just as you have danced with the women," Brown Hawk said as the steady beat of the drums again signaled the start of a new dance.

"My brother, I am so proud of you and also of you, Young Eagle," Little Flower sweetly said. This time Little Flower bravely looked at Young Eagle and smiled. Both suddenly felt the flutter of butterflies and both knew that the bread made of corn eaten many hours ago was not the reason.

Chapter Six

Warriors, both seasoned with many battles to brag of and the young who had yet to face any battle, walked toward the circle. The drum beat was soft and slow. The Hillabee Micco moved forward to the center of the circle. As they had many hours earlier in the day, all of the Hillabee people became silent, their attention directed to the Micco. No one had expected more speeches and if this was the case, surely the words would be of importance.

"My people," the Hillabee Micco said loudly. "Please excuse this intrusion in our celebration, but our leader Hothlepoya has received news this night which he thinks should be shared with each of you." Just as he stepped into the center of the circle of the anxious Hillabee people, a cool wind began to blow and the sound of a screech owl from the distant hills began its shrill piercing cry. Hothlepoya stood in silence, just as his people did, every adult felling an instant moment of dread, a sense of dark forbearing. The Hillabee people, as well as all Creek people, were very superstitious. They wondered if the owl's cry had anything to do with the leader's upcoming words.

"My people, again I ask you to forgive me for interrupting the festivities of the night." He paused as the call of the owl became louder and the town people began talking softly among themselves. "I fear the call of the owl is an ominous warning for the future. Word has come to me this night that the white fathers in Washington will send a white man, an agent he is called, here to teach the poor red man how they should live." Murmurs of disapproval arose from the large group of Hillabee people. "It seems now that the white fathers," with obvious contempt in his strong voice, he continued, "think the red people should live as the whites. They should learn to use the plow and the loom, no longer to go on the hunt and to no longer live as our grandfathers have lived for generations."

Angry shouts from warriors young and old now filled the air, the women began the shrill keening sound which had been made by native women for eons of time. Hothlepoya allowed the angry emotions voiced by his people to continue for a brief while before he held his large hand up, indicating silence. "When the day was still young and I spoke with you, my people, I said we will watch and we will wait. This agent, by the name of Hawkins, Benjamin Hawkins, will come to our land in several moons. The new leaves will have turned brown and fallen to the ground and the small streams will once again be glazed with ice. He will come and we will listen and we will watch and we will, when the time is right, be ready." More shouts were heard from the warriors who were ready at that moment to do whatever their war leader asked. "I warn you now to use caution and do not allow yourselves to be pulled into the trap of the white man. Do not give them any reason to say you are the blame for problems that will arise. Remember this, we the Hillabee and the Oakfuskee and all of the Creek people between the waters of the Oakfuskee and the Coosa … will be ready. Now, there is one dance remaining for this night and I think we should begin." Hothlepoya finished his talk not fully realizing the ominous portent of the screech owl and what the future would hold for his people.

Chapter Seven

The rapid beat of the drum began as warriors of all ages headed for the dance circle. A well seasoned veteran warrior with many notches in the bone handle of his knife suddenly yelled into the crowd, "We will be ready!" With that the dance began.

The warrior's dance that transpired for the next hour fully expressed the feelings of the Hillabee men. The dance of war as it was called, allowed the warriors to portray the actions during battle. Round and round they went with knives flashing in the firelight and the war clubs held high above their heads. Sounds of the war chants filled the night and the cool wind chilled the warriors, each one drenched in sweat.

Young Eagle and Brown Hawk, as did each and every warrior dancing, felt a deep stirring emotion, an emotion that had been experienced by many generations of warriors when their way of life had been threatened. The threat now was a formidable foe, one that would persist. This one the Hillabee warriors could not fathom; this one could not be defeated.

The warrior dance ended and the town people were bid a good night and told to go to their huti. Little Flower and Spotted Fawn left the square ground with their families. A strange, unfamiliar silence had fallen over the Hillabee people. No one, not even the sleepy, fussy children spoke. An eerie moon was high in the night sky and the chilling sound of the screech owl could once again be heard. The owl seemed be flying into the village, the sound louder and louder. The women pulling their children closer began to run toward their hutis. The men reaching for their knives were ready to defend themselves and their families from whatever unseen enemy was lurking nearby. Just as suddenly, as it had appeared, the owl and its blood curdling cry were gone. The men, normally fearless, were now completely shaken. Making sure the women and children were safe inside the huti, they talked softly among themselves.

"What can this mean," one of them asked. "Evil spirits have

entered into the village," another answered. "When the sun rises in the sky, we must go up White Oak Creek where the cedar trees grow. We must cut many branches and place them all around the town. We must protect ourselves from this evil."

The belief that branches of cedar would ward away evil and evil spirits did work for the Creek people, or they thought it did. The ominous warning of the events that would happen in the future could not be prevented by the branch of a cedar or even thousands of cedar trees, but this they did not know.

Chapter Eight

The morning sun had already rose high in the sky before Little Flower awoke to the sound of loud talking near the huti of her family. Realizing she was the only one remaining inside, she quickly dressed and braided her long black hair, pulling her moccasins on as she went outside. "My mother, I" … Little Flower began but was silenced by the serious look on her mother's face and her sudden signal for no speaking. Louder, angry words could be heard from the other side of the village, as well as the strong voice of her father's brother, the Hillabee Micco.

"We will do as our leader Hothlepoya has said. We will watch and we will wait and we will be ready." Little Flower knew her uncle, while not having the power to tell his warriors what they could do and not do, had their respect and they would listen. "We are not ready and the time is not yet right. I ask you now to go to your huti, to sleep off the bad effects of the firewater you seemed to have had too much of last night." Realizing he had the attention of the little group of rowdy young warriors and their urge to find white people to attack had quailed, the micco, as he always did, used his gift of diplomacy, stating "Or perhaps a long swim in the White Oak Creek would help to cool hot heads. Seriously, young warriors of Hillabee Town, we need for you to stay calm and I beg you not to make trouble for us now. The time, one day will be right and we will be ready and we will need you then. I am hungry now. I am going to my huti to eat and then I will go up White Oak Creek to help the others cut the branches of the cedar."

Sunflower Woman then looked at Little Flower and smiled. "As always, your uncle had calmed the young warriors. Now, what were you saying? I am glad you have decided not to sleep this day away. We have much work to do."

"My mother, I am sorry. I did not mean to sleep so long. I know I have my work to do." Little Flower said as she turned away, "but it looks as if someone has already begun it for me.

Mother, what was all the fuss about?"

"It seems that a few of the young warriors dipped a little too deep into the firewater bottle of trader Grierson last night and they were ready to find some white people to attack." Sunflower Woman said as she prepared Little Flower's bowl of sofkee.

"Mother, my brother and Young Eagle were not among the warriors were they?" Little Flower asked, afraid of what the answer would be.

"No, your brother and Young Eagle were not among the group, but the brother of your friend, Spotted Fawn was. His mother is very upset and fears that her son will become a trouble maker."

"May I go to their huti now? I know Fawn is worried too." Little Flower asked as she finished her sofkee.

"No, you may not." Sunflower Woman spoke sharply to her daughter. "The sun is now high in the sky and you, my child, have much work to do. Remember how good the meat of the deer was yesterday? It is now time for us to tan the hide of that deer." Smiling at Little Flower "we both will go and see our friends later."

Both mother and daughter spent the next several hours in the laborious task of removing hair from the hide of the deer. The skin had already been soaked overnight in the creek to make the removal easier and it had been placed over the log frame to begin the scraping process. Little Flower used a stone scraper while her mother used a knife that her husband had secured in trade with Mr. Gierson. This was only the first process as the skin would then need to be dried and soaked overnight in water.

Standing to stretch her legs, Sunflower Woman said to Little Flower, "This is all we can do today, tomorrow before the sun is so high," this in reference to Little Flower's late morning of sleep, "We will begin the next process of making the skin soft."

"My mother, why is this work of the women? The men have

stronger hands and the job would be much easier for them," Little Flower said as she cleaned her hands. "And I know tomorrow's work will be even harder as we stretch and pull and," making a face to indicate displeasure in what she would need to do, "also chew the skin and apply the brains of the deer to make it soft. This is not pleasant!"

"Little Flower, you are a young woman of the Hillabee and you are of the Wind Clan. I believe you already know the answer to that question," Sunflower Woman said sharply. "I am disappointed in my daughter and especially after I allowed you to dance with the women last night. Are you interested in becoming a woman or would you rather remain and be treated like a young child?"

"My mother, again I say that I am sorry. I no longer want to be treated as a child. I am proud to be a Hillabee of the Wind Clan and I do understand the work of the Creek woman is hard and that many grandmothers have done such work and that it is our responsibility to our people," Little Flower said, her brown eyes filling with tears.

"Little Flower, you must learn not to be so quick to shed tears. While the life of a Hillabee woman is good and we have many wonderful events to make us happy, we also have hard times that we must endure. We must be strong both in will and body and we cannot cry every time we think we have done wrong or we feel someone has spoken to strongly," Sunflower Woman said as she gathered the tools used to tan the deer skin. "I fear the days in your future may require even more strength and I want you to learn to be strong. Now, it is time for us to prepare food for your father and brother. They will return soon from their trip up White Oak Creek and they will want to eat."

"Mother, thank you for teaching me to be a strong Hillabee woman, I will learn quickly, but please tell me what you fear for me, what is going to be different?"

Several minutes passed before Sunflower Woman spoke. Little Flower thought her mother had not heard her question or was not planning to answer her. Sunflower Woman was busy adding more corn to the sofkee pot when she slowly raised her head and turned toward Little Flower. "My daughter, listen to me and keep these things in your heart. The happy lives the Hillabee and all of the tribes of our people are now living will not continue. This change will not happen soon, but before you have seen as many seasons as I, no longer will our people be allowed to live on this land that has been the home of our grandmother's grandmother, and even the time before that."

"But why, mother," Little Flower asked. Before her question could be answered, the loud voices of the men could be heard returning to the village. Each man carried many branches of green cedar, the pungent odor rapidly filling the air.

"Before the sun sets on this day, my child, you will know," Sunflower Woman predicted. "Let us now go help the men."

Chapter Nine

The men stopped at the village entrance, each depositing their load of cedar branches. The women and older children all gathered around the men, knowing that their responsibility would be to take the branches to their own huti. This was a familiar routine, one that had happened many times before when the chilling sound of the owl had been heard near the village.

This time seemed to be different, the men being in no hurry to leave even though the walk had been far and stomachs were empty. The women sensed words needed to be said and stopped the children from gathering the branches.

The husband of Sunflower Woman stepped forward and taking a branch of cedar from the pile, he turned to face the anxious group. "My people of the Hillabee, please listen well to my words. Today, as we traveled, the sound of the owl traveled with us. If we slowed our walk, the owl slowed his flight and if we ran, the owl would fly to the next bend and was there waiting with his mournful cry of death." The women sighed in fright and a few began their keening. "We do not know the meaning of this. We do not know if this evil is among us now or if this is a warning for the future." The strong warrior stopped speaking and he slowly looked into the faces of his people. His eyes rested on his family. "This is not all. As we traveled today, we met many others who had heard the cry of the owl. One of the warriors spoke of hearing about new white families moving near the homes of our people. One prophet we met on the trail said the cry of the owl is a warning to us. We must be ready, for evil is coming in the form of the white race who wish to take our homes and our land. Women, take your children and gather the branches of the cedar. Go to your huti and place them over the entrance and ask the Great Spirit to deliver us from the evil of the people whose skin is as white as frost on the ground during the moon of no leaves."

The women and children gathered their share of the cedar

branches, the fragrance still fresh and pungent. The families walked to their individual huti, each one silent and in thought of the words just spoken, the early spring sun warm on their backs with only a slight chill to remind them of the departing winter.

Sunflower Woman and Little Flower arrived at their huti only moments before Brave Hunter and Brown Hawk returned. Both father and son went directly to the clay bottles filled with fresh spring water and then to the iron pot of sofkee. Filling their bowls with simmering corn soup and picking up pieces of bread made from corn, Brave Hunter and Brown Hawk sat down on the couch-like seats bordering the wall of the huti.

"My wife and daughter," Brave Hunter said as he wiped moisture from his brown face. "Come and sit with us. There are words that must be spoken, words that come from my heart which could not be spoken before the Hillabee people."

Sunflower Woman and Little Flower went and sat near the feet of Brave Hunter. Neither questioned the request which seemed so strange to both of them. Brown Hawk followed the lead of his father and placed the bowl of sofkee to his side. He had heard the words of the Keethla-Knower and had seen the crystal turn from clear to gray as the man who had seen many seasons, predicted the future of the Hillabee people.
"We met another man on the trail today, a Keethla from the lower Oakfuskee town of Tuckabatchee. He told us of the uncertain times his town is experiencing. Many of his people are eager to accept the wares of the trader just as the Hillabee have. Some of their neighbors from across-the-river town of Talisi are moving their families up Eufaubee Creek. He said that he had made the long trip down the Alabama to the place where that big river joins the one the Choctaw people call the Tombigbee." Brave Hunter paused and drank water from his clay cup, his demeanor becoming sad and forlorn. "He saw many white people there, not just men with trades, but entire families. Trees were being cut down and houses were being built.

The Keethla told us that he pulled his divining crystal from his pouch and softly asked, "What is the meaning of this, will a time soon come when there are more white people here than red, will they take from us the land of our people, will they kill the women and children as well as the brave warriors who try to defend them?" Brave Hunter again paused, this time several minutes passed before he spoke. His wife and children sat quietly looking at the man they knew and loved, realizing the pain he was experiencing was deep and real. They also knew what he would say next. Brave Hunter continued, "The sun was bright with no cloud to hide the light, the crystal sparkled brilliantly clear and then in a blink of his eye, the knower saw the shining rock turn dark grey with streaks of red running from top to bottom. He had the answer to his question. The knower told me that in each village he visited, the result was the same.

This morning I saw myself as he asked the question, "Will the white man take the land of the Hillabee people?" My family, the beautiful crystal turned an ugly gray with the streaks of red, the color of blood. This is the blood of our people."

Sunflower Woman could no longer control herself and her loud keening filled the huti. Little Flower began to cry, her brother looking as if he too would allow tears to flow, but instead, jumped up shouting, "My father, I will not allow this to happen. I will fight to the death for my town and my people."

Chapter Ten

The silence was heavy in the huti as the family, each in their own way, digested the revelation of the future for the Hillabee people. Evening shadows had begun to spread over the top of the trees and the cool wind once again chilled the air, indicating that the day would soon turn to the darkness of night.

Sunflower Woman was the first to break the long period of silence, realizing that she had much work to finish before darkness covered the town. "Little Flower, we must get busy, move along now, quickly go to the spring and fill the water bottles and gather more branches for the fire. Your father and brother will need a hearty meal of more than sofkee."

Brave Hunter stood, his tall frame almost touching the top of the huti. "My wife, we must place the cedar branches over the entrance and around our huti. This must be done before the evening work and before we can eat. Brown Hawk and I will help with this. We will work together, just as we and all of our people will work together for the good of the Hillabee."

"Yes, my husband, we will work together and the Great Spirit, the Giver of Breath, will help us to accomplish this." Sunflower Woman said as she opened the skin flap that served as a door. Many were busy, arranging cedar branches around their huti while others were doing their routine evening jobs. The village was subdued and everyone seemed to be doing their work quickly as if to beat the darkness that was closing in on the Hillabee town.

"Brown Eagle, go with your sister to the spring that runs into the creek and bring some of the broken sticks for the fire. I will help your mother finish with the cedar. We need to all be inside before darkness falls." Brave Hunter said to his son, knowing that what he asked was normally the work of the women.

"Yes, my father, I will do this. We will return soon."

When the brother and sister had left the huti to gather

firewood and get the water, Sunflower Woman turned to her husband with a concerned look on her still beautiful face. "Are there more words that should be said, is there some evil that we should fear now and not just in the future?"

"My wife, my beautiful Sunflower," Brave Hunter said as he pulled her close to him. "I do not know. I have a strange feeling that much sadness is to come to us and to all of our people. I believe what the Keethla has predicted will happen. I hope many seasons will first pass before we will need to fight the white people, but it will happen. I fear for our children. What will become of them if our way of life is no longer the same? Also, the Keethla said there are more reasons we should be aware and cautious. He said evil spirits and witches are restless now and may cause us harm."

"My husband, what can we do to keep these spirits away from us?" Sunflower Woman asked as fear began to rise within her. She and the Hillabee as well as all Creek people were superstitious, believing in and greatly fearing evil spirits, ghost and people who could turn into witches.

"We will be strong and ask again for the Giver of Breath to protect us," Brave Hunter said as he tenderly kissed his wife.

Chapter Eleven

Brown Hawk and Little Flower swiftly walked down the path next to White Oak Creek. Each carrying a clay water bottle to fill with clear water from the spring which bubbled over the rocks into the creek.

"Hawk," using the shortened name she often called her brother, Little Flower breathlessly said, "I am afraid. Can we please hurry? It soon will be dark and there is no moon to show us the way."

"Flower, I too am uncomfortable. We are almost at the spring and we will be on our way back to our huti before much time passes."

"Hear, Brown Hawk, let me help." The familiar voice of Young Eagle was heard over the rushing stream. He took the jar from Little Flower and bent down to fill it with water, and then hurriedly filled the other one Brown Hawk was holding. "Let us go now. We can pick up sticks along the way."

"Thank you Young Eagle." Brown Hawk said. "Little Flower is frightened and I too would like to get back to our huti before blackness covers the sky."

The three walked rapidly back toward the village. Little Flower stumbled and Young Eagle grabbed her arm to prevent her from falling. Suddenly, as the twilight turned into night, the cool wind began to blow and the chilling sound heard the night before filled the air. The owl flew from tree to tree, just barely over the heads of Young Eagle and Brown Hawk. Shadows seemed to float just ahead as the youths ran. Never had the path from the spring seemed so long.

Firelight from the camp fires were a welcoming sight as Young Eagle, Brown Hawk and Little Flower entered the village. Others had heard the owl; some saying there was more than one. The shapes and shadows had been seen by several of the women as they too had hurried to finish the evening work.

Little Flower was visibly shaken, barely containing the tears that threatened to fall. Young Eagle was still holding on to her hand, having taken it as they ran down the path. He realized this and slowly released it as the village sprang to life in response to the commotion.

"My children, what happened? Are you hurt?" Sunflower Woman asked as she and Brave Hunter rushed outside the huti.

"We are not hurt my mother, but we have seen things we are not sure of and Little Flower…" Brown Hawk paused and then said, "All of us were frightened."

"What did you see?" Brave Hunter asked. Many of the village people had gathered around the huti of Sunflower Woman, wanting to know what had happened. Others who had witnessed the strange occurrence remained silent, waiting to hear what Brown Hawk and Young Eagle had to say. The young warriors looked at each other, both willing the other to speak first. Young Eagle, seemingly the more composed, spoke.

"Father of my friend, I will begin at the beginning. I, too, had gone down the path to the spring. I heard the voices of my friend and his sister. Darkness was quickly descending and I knew we would need to hurry. We filled the water jars and had gathered sticks for the fire. We had turned to make our way back to the village when again we heard the mournful cry of the owl, just as we had last night. This time the owl flew barely above our heads, so close we could have reached up and touched it."

The Hillabee people stood in silence for a brief period. Then one of the women who had been gathering firewood near the village stepped forward saying, "Did you see anything else, something you could not identify?"

"Yes, we did," Brown Hawk said. "Little Flower, Young Eagle and I all saw shapes and forms that seemed at first to be real and then disappear only to be seen again further up the path."

"One seemed to be that of a woman who laughed and then another that made the sad sound of a woman in grief," Little Flower said, feeling more at ease now that she was in the safety of her village.

"I too saw these things," the woman said, "but one of them pointed a finger at me. Oh! I am so frightened. What does it mean?"

No one had any answer to the woman's question. No one could explain the presence of the shapes that the young warriors, Little Flower and others had seen that night. The people of the Hillabee village were nervous for the next few days. Some looked over their shoulder every time they entered into the wooded area around the huti, expecting to see the floating shapes or hear the owl. Many did see things which could not be explained and the owl continued to make nightly excursions throughout the town. Some of the old beloved men said these things were evil omens of events that would happen in the future. Others thought the owls and shapes were not evil at all but were, in fact, spirits of the ancestors lighting the path of change for the Hillabee, and in time that change would come.

While no one forgot the strange happenings, the daily life did return to normal for the Hillabee town. The rays of the sun warmed the earth and the women and children prepared the ground for planting of the beans and corn. Instead of the ominous cry of the owl, the air was filled with the joyful sound of the flirting bluebird in search of its mate.

The men went on the spring hunt bringing back the turkey which provided the much needed meat, as well as the feathers the women would use in so many ways. Repairs were made to the huti and the women and children ventured down White Oak Creek where the sloping banks provided the colorful red and orange clay used to form the bowls and bottles for daily needs. Some of the women planned to make new bowls with special designs that would be used during the Poskeeta.

The men continued to meet at the square ground outside the council house. Now that the nights were warmer there was no need to be inside. They drank the black drink and smoked their pipes. They talked of the owl and the shapes that moved without touching the ground. They talked of the rumors of more white people moving closer to their hunting grounds. They talked of ways to stop the tide of white intrusion into their lives. Some of them talked of the guns and hatchets received from the white traders that had made the hunt easier. Again, some of the old ones talked of the danger of embracing this new easier way of life and some talked of using the new weapons to retain the old way.

Even then, the difference of opinions was beginning to make small rifts between the people, rifts that would open the door for change. Just as the days of new leaves of the warm season had changed into the long days of the bountiful crop, change was coming for the Hillabee people.

Part Two
Hillabee Town
Time of the New Leaves, 1802

Chapter One

Six years had passed since the new leaf season of the owl. This was the name the Hillabee people now called the time the owls and images had made the unwanted visits to the village. This was still talked of during the time of story telling, the method used to preserve history of the people. Children hearing this for the first time would cling to their skirts of their mothers and even the older ones would hurry through the woods on dark nights. No one had been successful in providing an answer as to why the winged creatures of the night and the translucent figures had come to the Hillabee village. No one had suffered from any fatal illness, nor had any unexplained accidents occurred during or immediately after the visit, other than the close call when Little Flower slipped into the creek. Many still said these strange things were omens of some terrible event that would occur in the future.

Keeping this warning in their heart, the Hillabee people continued on with the daily routine of life. Crops were planted and harvested; men went on the hunt and continued to spend time in the council house and square ground. They continued to drink the accee and smoke their pipes. They continued to talk of white expansion near the homes of the Creek and many continued to talk of the new way of life the white people had introduced to the Hillabees.

Benjamin Hawkins, the government agent, had been sent to live among the southern native people and had visited the villages of the Hillabee many times. He praised them for accepting the new ways and listened while the old beloved men warned of the trouble this would create. Hawkins used trader Grierson and his Creek wife as an example of the successful life style that could be obtained if the Hillabee followed the way of the whites.

Trader Robert Grierson had lived among the Hillabee for thirty years, opening his trading house just across from the main village on Hillabee Creek. His was not the first trade the Hillabee had experienced. Many remembered hearing the talk of the grandfathers about the rum and colorful beads and trinkets that had been traded to the Hillabee in the past for the skins of the deer.

During that span of time between the first encounter with the trader and his goods and the present time, many if not most of the people enjoyed the easier life created by those goods. The result was a major change in the lifestyle for the Hillabee. Now, more was wanted in the exchange than the deer skin. Just as the beloved men who chose to live their lives in the old traditional way had predicted, the trader and the many other people who had followed, now wanted what was most precious to the Hillabee and other Creeks, they wanted their land.

This change had happened slowly without any realization of what was transpiring. The Hillabee had welcomed with open arms trader Grierson and his wife, Sinnugee, to the Hillabee town. She was, after all, a Creek and was one of them. She was of the Spanalgee Clan, one that the Hillabee people were not familiar with, but Sinnugee's home had been near the Savannah River and it might have been that things were different there. Many of the women, while doing their daily work tanning the deer hide, making the clay into pottery vessels or beating the corn in the stone mortars, talked of Sinnugee. Some said she was only part Creek, but also had the blood of the Shawnee. One of the older women who had traveled south with her husband to the towns in Spanish Florida, said she had the look of the Spanish.

It mattered little as to which clan or tribe Sinnugee belonged, to the Hillabee women she was their sister. She and her eight children, all of whom had been born at Hillabee town, helped with the Grierson enterprise, which was quite extensive. Not only did trader Grierson have the trading post, but he and his family farmed many acres of prime land along Hillabee Creek. In addition to the usual vegetable crops the Hillabee grew, the Grierson's planted rice and cotton, probably the first to be grown in the Tallapoosa River Valley. A favorite of the Hillabee people were the peaches from Grierson's orchard. Grierson also introduced cattle and horses to the area.

Being quite industrious, Trader Grierson created the factory system in the valley. With the success of the cotton crop, the cotton needed to be ginned and the trader brought the first cotton gin into the Creek Nation. He also saw the advantage of making cooking oil from the hickory nuts and acorns that covered the forest floor near Hillabee village. Many of the Hillabee women and children helped in some way or the other, either on the farm or in the cooking oil process by first gathering and then cracking and cooking the nuts. Others helped Sinnugee spin or weave cloth from the cotton. In this way, the Creek family was learning the ways of the white man.

Chapter Two

Little Flower, now a beautiful young woman, approaching her nineteenth season of new leaves, combed and braided her long black hair. She still lived in the huti of her mother, although many of her friends had become wives and had huti of their own.

Sunflower Woman was, as were all Creek women, very strong both in body and spirit, but since the season of the owl, she seemed to have lost some of her spirit. Little Flower had suspected that her mother was with child and a few days after the owl's visit to the town, Sunflower Woman had gone to the big huti of the women. When she returned, Little Flower learned that her mother had lost the baby she had so desperately wanted. She had over the years lost several, having only Little Flower and her brother, Brown Hawk. Sun Flower Woman had tried to be brave and accept the faith the Giver of Breath had chosen for her, but many times she had felt much sorrow in her heart. She had an unexplainable feeling that she had failed her people. There would need to be many children if they were to survive the influx of whites.

She knew her daughter would soon leave the safety and comfort her parents provided and turn to the arms of her husband. This brought both sad and happy emotions to Sunflower Woman but she was ready now for this change and smiled as she watched her daughter slip her feet into her tiny moccasins.

"Mother, I have finished my morning work and now I am going across White Oak Creek to work with Sinnugee," Little Flower said. "I am learning well how to weave the cotton into cloth." She paused, thinking what she would like to make from the cloth. "Sinnugee said that I may have, for my work, a piece big enough to make a dress like the one she wears."

Sunflower Woman noticed that her daughter no longer asked if she could go, but instead had told of her plans. "That is well, Little Flower, but please return home before darkness falls. Do you also plan to talk with Soaring Eagle today?" After the events of Little Flower's fall into the creek and the owl visit to the town, Young Eagle had received his warrior name. Now known as Soaring Eagle, he had become respected for his bravery and for the goodness of his heart. The Hillabee knew that he would become a good leader in the not too distant future. He and Little Flower had become close friends, the two of them and Brown Hawk, who was now known as Brave Hawk, had spent much time together. Brave Hawk too had gained the respect of his people, making more excuses to be alone with the friend of his sister, Spotted Fawn. Little Flower knew the time was approaching when her brother and her friend would be married. She also knew that she and Soaring Eagle would soon share the same huti.

"Yes, mother, I will talk with Soaring Eagle today, but I will return home before the darkness comes. I will also fill the water bowl with fresh water and bring in sticks for the fire. My mother, what will you do this day, could you not come with me? Sinnugee has much work to be done and many of our women help her and we can always use more of the brightly colored beads. I think I need, I mean…" Little Flower quickly covered the mistaken word as a slight flush covered her beautiful face; "I would like to have more white ones."

"My, how quickly your words come today," Sunflower Woman said as she hugged her daughter. "To answer the first of your questions, I will travel with your father down the creek to Oktasassi town. He has words to say to the Big Beloved Man. This will allow me to see the wife of my brother and some of my friends, and you know, my daughter, that I will not work for the wife of trader Grierson. Your father and I agree with many of the Hillabee people on this subject. While we do understand that some of the items received in trade are good and have made our lives easier, we also realize that our people are depending too much on the white man and his trade goods." Sunflower Woman stopped speaking and a look of sadness filled her brown eyes. "Little Flower do you remember the time of the owl?"

"Of course I do mother." Little Flower replied as she sat back down on the couch that lined the huti wall. She knew that her mother had words to say, words she knew she should hear. "I will never forget that time."

"Remember what I told you? I said change was coming for our people. Just in the few seasons since the owl came to our village, much change has taken place. In the early time when the trader first came, the people saw the beads and trinkets and they liked them, but these were things we did not need and did not have to have. As seasons went by, the trader offered the metal axe and the iron pot which replaced our stone tools and pots made from clay. Soon our warriors all wanted the musket and balls to hunt the deer and also to kill their enemy." Sunflower Woman sat down in the front of Little Flower, the sunlight from the open door shinning directly on her face, creating a glow around the beautiful Creek woman who now spoke with so much emotion. "The trader did not want any of the finely crafted arrows or tools our men had made and they had no use for any of the beautiful clay pots our women had spent much time in making. Little Flower, you know the reason that your father, your brother, Soaring Eagle and all of the other warriors of our town spent so much time on the hunt was not for food for us to eat, but for the deer skin to use for trade. Now, the deer are almost gone and our men have to go farther and farther on the hunt just to find enough for our needs. With every new season that comes, there seem to be more and more white families traveling near the Creek land and some of these people think they can take our land for their own." Tears were now forming in the eyes of Sunflower Woman. "Oh, my daughter, I fear for you and Soaring Eagle and for the children that you will be blessed with by the Great Spirit. I know the talk of battles and fighting between the Red Man and the White will soon become more than talk. Little Flower, my heart is filled with sadness. What will happen to you…what will happen to all of the Hillabee?"

Little Flower looked at her mother, again feeling that

some of the great strength and spirit Sunflower Woman once possessed had been drained from her. Little Flower was also surprised to hear her mother speak of Soaring Eagle and their children. What did she know of their relationship and the great love she had for him? "My mother, please do not fear for me or the Hillabee people. We are strong. We will keep our home and our land. I understand now why you will not work for Sinnugee. You see the influence she is having on our people. You are right; some of the Hillabee are living more like the white families who want our land. Mother, I will not work for her either," Little Flower said, trying to hide the disappointment she felt. She knew of no other way to obtain the cloth and white beads she would use to make the dress she would need in the future. "My mother," she paused briefly, trying to say the correct words, "you said something about my children and Soaring Eagle, what … I mean, how do you …"

The expression on Sunflower Woman's face suddenly changed from sadness to that of joy. "My child, do you think I have no eyes to see and no ears to hear? I know the two of you share much love and I know that this too began at the time of the owl. I also know there will be a wedding celebration soon."

"The mother of Soaring Eagle has already spoken to your aunt and grandmother about this and you know the special feeling I have for him. He did save the life of my child on the day the owl came. He is the best friend of your brother and all of the people of the Hillabee town have much respect for him."

"Mother, does this mean that you approve of my marriage to Soaring Eagle," Little Flower asked, with tears forming in her eyes.

"Yes, you silly child, and your father will be very proud to call Eagle his son, but you do realize we expect you to be married in the Creek way and the proper plans should continue to be made with me, my sister and your grandmother." Sunflower Woman stood and kissed her daughter on her cheek as she brushed away the little tears that fell from Little Flower's doe-like eyes. "Your father is waiting for me down by the creek.

The sun will be low in the sky before we return. I need for you to have fresh soffkee in the pot and if you return in time, after working for the wife of Trader Grierson, please have the bread made from the dried corn ready to place on the fire."

"Mother, I know that I should not work for Sinnugee. I will find other ways…"

"Little Flower," Sunflower Woman said softly, how else will you get the cloth and beads for the dress you will soon wear? You are intelligent and I know you understand the difference between being a Creek woman and being white. Go now, and save some of the day to be with Soaring Eagle."

Chapter Three

Little Flower walked across the bridge made from logs that spanned Hillabee Creek and on down the path that led to the Grierson farm. She was surprised to see some of her friends and their mothers already hard at work. Some were in the shed-like areas where the looms were set up, while others gathered under the big oak trees near the big mortars, the sharp sound of the nuts being cracked could be heard as she approached them. She also noticed that many of her closest friends were not present and for the first time she realized why. Their mother or their husbands would not allow them to work for the Griersons. Sunflower Woman's talk had helped Little Flower to understand many things that were happening in the village and she could see the changes of which her mother had spoken.

Sinnugee saw Little Flower walk into the opening and was delighted to see her. She had hoped that the beautiful young woman would come. Little Flower always worked very hard and seemed to have an encouraging effect on the others. Everyone liked and respected her, although a few were jealous of the attention Soaring Eagle showed her. He was one of the most handsome and bravest young warriors in the village and some of the young women tried, in vain, to capture his interest. It was becoming more and more obvious to them that Little Flower had won his heart.

"Little Flower," Sinnugee said. "I am glad to see you this beautiful morning. Would you like to work with the loom? I think you may have the cloth you need if you will work hard today." Sinnugee realized the family of Little Flower did not participate in any of the farm or factory jobs the Grierson's offered. She was concerned that Little Flower would cease coming as well.

"Thank you, Sinnugee. Yes, I would like to use the loom." Little Flower said as she smiled at the others who stopped their work only briefly to acknowledge her. She also saw the scene differently. Little Flower saw the women working hard for Sinnugee and their payment would only be a few beads, or a little of the rum which made the warriors act as crazy as the fox. A few, like her, if they worked many long days, might receive a small piece of cloth made from the cotton. Remembering again the words her mother had said only a short time ago, Little Flower fully understood now. Sinnugee and her family were the benefactors of this work done by the Hillabee women. Why were they working for someone else when there was much work to be done for their own family? Little Flower said softly to herself, "Why am I here, is it so important to me to have cloth so that I might be like the white woman?" Slowly stepping away from the loom, Little Flower turned to go.

"Where are you going Little Flower?" Sinnugee asked, already knowing the answer. "Do you not want to work today? Do you not want your cloth you have earned?"

"Sinnugee," Little Flower stood as tall as her small body would allow and suddenly feeling the Spirit of generations of Wind Clan grandmothers within her, she proudly said, "I am a Hillabee woman of the Wind Clan. I do not need or want the cloth of the white man. On the day of celebration when I become the wife of Soaring Eagle, I will wear, like my grandmothers before me, the soft skin of the deer. Sinnugee, you are my friend, but I will not return here to work for you. If there are things I need, I or my father will come to the trading house and fair trades will be made. I will go now."

Not surprised by the strong statement made by the young woman, Sinnugee was still saddened to see her go and not to come again. "Little Flower, I will not try to prevent you from leaving, but I am sorry that your feelings have changed about working here for me." Sinnugee said as she turned to go inside a large huti used for storage where the items of payment were kept. "You have worked many days for me and I owe you for that work. It can not be said that Sinnugee Grierson does not pay for work done. I think you will be beautiful in a dress made from the soft skin of a deer that you tan yourself. I hope you will accept these beads," she said as she handed Little Flower a small skin pouch filled with white beads. "I know you will need these to complete your dress."

"I will accept the beads Sinnugee, as you said, I have worked and should have payment and the beads are all that I need," Little Flower said as she took the pouch from Sinnugee. "I will not work for you again, but I will come across the creek to see you and on the day of celebration, I hope you and your family will come," Little Flower said as she turned to leave the work area. Little Flower did not realize that each of the Hillabee women had stopped their work and were watching the actions and hearing the conversation between the older woman and the spirited younger one. As she approached the log bridge Little Flower heard footsteps behind her. Turning to see who was following so closely, she was surprised to see two women and four of their daughters.

"Wait, Little Flower," one of the women said. "We will no longer work here and we no not want to be like white women. We will return to the village and do the work that waits for us there. Thank you for showing us the way."

Little Flower smiled at the group of Hillabee women. "The Spirit of the grandmothers has guided all of us this day."

Chapter Four

Little Flower and the other Hillabee women crossed the creek and each went to their own huti. Little Flower placed the beads Sinnugee had given her for the work done in the special pouch that contained the other items she prized. Knowing that Sunflower Woman would not be back until later in the day, she decided to walk along the smaller creek to the meadow where she and Soaring Eagle often met. He would not be there now, the sun was still too high in the sky, but she had much to think about. Little Flower had a feeling of pride in herself for leaving the farm of Sinnugee. She knew her father and mother would be proud too. She was also happy that her action had influenced others to do the same. Why had she not realized long ago that working for the Grierson family was helping to bring change to the Hillabee people, the change her mother had talked of many times. The change the beloved men had said was to come during the time of the owl. Everything was clear now; she had been working so that she could obtain the possessions of the white woman. Little Flower also understood the division that was beginning to form within the Hillabee people. Some of them had the same opinion and felt as she did while others desired the white man's way of life. Like her mother, she feared for the future of her people.

Little Flower continued walking until she arrived at the special place where she and Soaring Eagle had spent much time together. There they had talked of their future and the problems that faced the Hillabee people. Soaring Eagle, now being recognized as a brave warrior and having the potential for being a leader, was privileged to hear the words of the beloved men and the miccos. He felt strongly as they did, that the desire their people had for the white man's trade goods was growing and that many of them were letting go of the traditional way. Concerns of equal importance to Soaring Eagle and the leaders were the treaties which continued to give the white man more and more of the Creek land. Changing and troubling times were closing in on the Creek people.

Little Flower spread the red blanket she had carried with her between the two long leaf pines that bordered the creek. She leaned against one of the several huge granite stones, warm from the sun that filtered down through the trees. Behind the stones, the woods seemed to open creating a beautiful little meadow already dotted by the yellow and blue wild flowers that indicated the time of cold was over and the days would soon be long and warm.

The warm sunshine made her drowsy and comfortable and Little Flower slowly succumbed to the sleep that overcame her. She dreamed that she and Soaring Eagle were married and their child, a little girl that looked like her mother, was playing in front of their huti. In her dream, Little Flower was happy and content and all was well with her people. Then suddenly, the child screamed and the sound of the owl with its chilling cry of death was heard throughout the village. War whoops and sounds from a large gun filled the air. Little Flower awoke from her sleep and heard herself crying for her child.

She felt strong arms around her and smelled the familiar scent of Soaring Eagle. "Little Flower, my flower, why are you crying? Who is this child you are calling for?" Soaring Eagle asked as he pulled Little Flower close to him.

"Oh Soaring Eagle," Little Flower could not control the tears that streamed down her cheeks. "I dreamed we were married and of our child and…and the owl came again. There were warriors fighting everywhere and loud sounds that I have never heard before." Little Flower told Soaring Eagle the complete dream again and while she had stopped crying, she still was shaken by the dream which seemed so real.

"Little Flower, it was only a dream but I like the part about us being married." Soaring Eagle smiled. "But the owl and our warriors fighting does upset me too. Many of the beloved women have dreams which seem to predict the future. I will pray to the Great Spirit that you do not have that ability and that this dream does not come true." Soaring Eagle said as he gently wiped the tears from Little Flower's eyes and kissed her wet cheek. "Come, walk with me," he said as he took her hand and pulled her to her feet. "I have words to say that will chase the fear from your heart and make you happy."

"Just seeing you makes me happy, my Eagle," Little Flower said, using the endearing word of possession she called him when they were alone. "My mother and father have traveled down to Oktasassi Town, so we can walk far and enjoy this day of sunshine together. What words will you say to me, Eagle?"

"Little Flower," Soaring Eagle said, stopping and turning her to face him. "I realize that many of your friends already have husbands and some now have sons and daughters. Brave Hawk has told me that he will ask you to talk with the aunt of Spotted Fawn and her grandmother. The two of them will become one in the bond of marriage very soon."

"Oh, that is good! When did he plan to tell his mother and sister?" Little Flower asked, trying to act hurt because she did not yet know the plans of her brother.

"He plans to tell his family when he returns from his trip up river. That will be in two suns," Soaring Eagle said as he laughed at Little Flower.

"Why is he going up river?" Little Flower excitedly asked.

"The river mussels are big and there is also an oak tree filled with much honey that we will take before anyone else can. Also, there is a small village of the Cherokee people nearby. The women make their pottery bowls from different color clay. We will trade for some of this clay. It will make a good Hillabee bowl." Soaring Eagle said as he looked toward the blue sky as a large bird glided effortlessly in the wind. "Look Little Flower, the eagle has come to guide the way for me and to give me courage."

Little Flower was confused. She did not understand why Soaring Eagle would need guidance or courage. What was he saying?

Soaring Eagle seemed to pause as if he was at a loss for

words. He suddenly felt as frightened as a small boy on his first hunt. Taking a deep breath, Soaring Eagle lifted Little Flower's chin and looked deep into her brown eyes. "Brave Hawk is going up river to bring back gifts for the aunt and grandmother of Spotted Fawn. I am going for gifts for the family of Little Flower. It is time and I am ready for you to become the wife of Soaring Eagle." He paused, "if you are ready for Soaring Eagle to become your husband."

Many times Little Flower and Soaring Eagle had talked about the future and of their marriage. Little Flower had been ready, but she knew that Soaring Eagle was not and the time was not yet right. Soaring Eagle was spending much of his time with the old beloved men and micco of Hillabee Towns and those of other surrounding villages. He was to learn the way of these knowledgeable and experienced men. During the time of Poskeeta, Soaring Eagle was to have the honor and duty of becoming a Micco Apotka, he would become an assistant to the Hillabee micco. This position required the man to be responsible and married, no longer free to act as a young warrior.

"I am ready to become the wife of Soaring Eagle," Little Flower said as tears sparkled in her eyes.

Soaring Eagle picked up his future wife and spun her around until they both were dizzy. Feeling the excitement of their future together, he pulled her close and held her small body next to his. Letting Little Flower go, he placed a kiss on her forehead saying, "Now I must go meet your brother. We have far to go before the sun shines no longer on this day."

"Soaring Eagle, has your sister had words with my mother and grandmother as Creek way requires?"

"She has. That is the reason for the trip up river. The grandmother of Little Flower request large mussels and the clay from the Cherokee women. Sunflower Woman has asked for fresh honey. When I return, I will begin cutting wood for your huti and also we will break up new land to plant corn and beans. Then I will go on the hunt to supply us with meat. When that is done, you will be my wife and the day of celebration will begin." Soaring Eagle waved at his Little Flower as he turned to follow the path up the creek to meet with Brave Hawk.

Chapter Five

Little Flower could barely contain her excitement as she walked back to the village. She wished that her mother had returned from the trip to Oktasassi, but the sun was still high in the sky. She stopped and talked with many of the women as they did their daily work, helping them as they talked. Many inquired about her work at the Grierson Farm and were happy about her decision not to work there anymore. One of the older women, totally clad in the traditional way of the Creek, looked up at Little Flower as she finished etching the designs on her clay pot. Little Flower recognized her as being a sister of Soaring Eagle's grandmother. The woman, showing the signs of having seen many winters, smiled broadly at Little Flower.

"When this bowl has cooled from the fire, it will be a gift for you, my child. I wish for you to prepare sofkee many times for the grandson of my sister and I wish," the old woman suddenly broke into laughter as if she was remembering the times of her long ago youth, "for you to have many sons and daughters to fill your huti. I know you will make a good wife for Soaring Eagle."

Little Flower smiled at the old woman and thanked her for the gift. "How did you know that Soaring Eagle will be my husband?"

All of the women began laughing and Little Flower wondered if the entire village knew. One of the other women sitting in the circle leaned over and hugged her. "Little Flower, we have known since the time of the owl that you will be the wife of Soaring Eagle. We have plans for a big day of celebration and all of the pots and bowls we are making today will be yours."

"Since the time of the owl," Little Flower said in total confusion. "That has been many seasons ago and I was only a child. How could you know?"

Repeating the words of the mother of Little Flower, another of the women answered. "My child, do you think we have no eyes to see and no ears to hear? All of the Hillabee people share in the happiness for you and Soaring Eagle."

Chapter Six

As night was beginning to fall on the day of the second sun, Soaring Eagle and Brave Hawk returned to the Hillabee town. Both seemed to be in an agitated state and went directly to the square ground where the men had retired to smoke their pipes. Little Flower saw them enter the village and realized their urgency to speak with the Hillabee micco.

After what seemed to be an endless time, both her brother, father and future husband came to the huti of her mother. As was the Creek custom, all three men went directly to the pot of sofkee and filled the clay bowls. After satisfying their hunger, they settled down near the fire. Both women waited impatiently for one of the men to speak. Just when Little Flower was about to break the silence herself, Soaring Eagle, smiling for the first time since entering the village, looked at the women. "My Flower, I know of the curiosity that bubbles within you and that you are now ready to hear my words." Nodding in agreement, Little Flower sat down across from Soaring Eagle and listened closely as he spoke.

"As you know, Brave Hawk and I both had reason to journey up the Oakfuskee River", smiling again at Little Flower, Soaring Eagle continued. "And yes, all that we were in search of was secured," his face again becoming serious. "We also found out many things that disturbed us. The people of the Cherokee have received news from their old home in the land called Georgia. Some of their people have again given in to the demand of the white man for more of their land. Also, many of the Cherokee people, just as the Creek have, are becoming comfortable with the white way of life and they are letting go of the old traditional ways." Soaring Eagle stopped speaking, sadness covering his strong, handsome face.

As Brave Hawk listened to the words of his friend, his normally fun-filled demeanor changed to one of seriousness as he said, "The Cherokee told us that some of their people were leaving the Cherokee land to live in a different place, a place across a big river, far away from the land of their grandfathers."

The father of Little Flower, speaking for the first time, strongly added. "The land of the father of my grandfather must always be my home. I will fight to the end before I will leave."

The group sat in silence, each pondering the words that had been said. The huti seemed to be filled with sadness for the future of the Hillabee people. Suddenly, as if he could no longer contain the energy and excitement within him, Brave Hawk jumped to his feet and grabbed his leather pouch. "My family and my friend, I have others to see before the moon rises in the sky."

Little Flower, always eager to have fun with her brother, could not resist laughing as she asked, "Is my brother planning to see the mother and aunt of Spotted Fawn?"

Soaring Eagle too seemed ready to joke with his friend, saying, "Or is it Spotted Fawn you wish to see this night?"

Never letting the words of his sister or his friend, who was more like a brother, upset him, he laughed as well. "The two of you should come with me and see," Brave Hawk said as he pulled Little Flower up from her knelling position. "Good night my mother, my father, I will see you in the square after the sun rises on the new day."

"My mother, I am going to walk with Soaring Eagle. I have many questions to ask him. I will return before the moon is very high in the sky." Little Flower said as she and Soaring Eagle left the huti.

Sunflower Woman smiled at her husband as the three young people left the huti. She knew it would only be a short time before her daughter would no longer tell of her plans or return to the huti of her mother. The thought of this made her heart both sad and happy at the same time. Brave Hawk had lived in the large huti of the unmarried warriors for several seasons and no longer considered this one his home, unless he was hungry. Sunflower Woman knew also that her son planned to become the husband of Spotted Fawn and that she would provide the sofkee to fill his stomach.

"My husband, the seasons of our life are quickly passing us by. Our son will soon become a husband and our daughter will soon become a wife and they too will have sons and daughters of their own." Sunflower Woman said as her eyes filled with tears.

"My wife, why does this make you cry? Do you not want to hold your grandchildren and teach them the way of the Hillabee people?" Brave Hunter asked as he tenderly pulled her near him. He was concerned about his wife. Tears filled her beautiful eyes more often now and her spirit did not seem as strong as it had in her youth.

"Yes, this makes me happy to think of holding my grandchildren, but will I be allowed to teach them the Hillabee way? Will the way of our people still be our way or will our people live as the whites?" Sunflower Woman asked.

"My wife, our grandchildren will know the way of our people, the Hillabee people, and the Creek people. I will see to this and for as long as I live, this land will be our home and their home."

Sunflower Woman cried herself to sleep in the arms of her husband and did not know that the moon was indeed high in the night sky before her daughter quietly removed her moccasins and slipped under the blanket on her couch.

Chapter Seven

The rays of the early morning sun seemed to smile on the Hillabee people as they began the work of the new day. Children were sent to gather firewood and fill water bottles while the women began preparing the morning meal. The men, as soon as their stomachs were filled, would convene at the square ground. The disturbing words of Soaring Eagle and Brave Hawk from the night before must be discussed. More news had come from the down river town of Tuckabatchee and of how agent Hawkins had continued to teach and urge the people there to accept the new, easy way of life. Just as disturbing to many of the elders and old beloved men, were the number of their people who saw no wrong in this new way of life.

Little Flower seemed to beam as she helped her mother with the morning work. She and Soaring Eagle had sat by the creek long into the night. First, listening to the sounds of the chirping tree frogs and far off yelp of the coyotes, and then talking of their future.

This would be the day Soaring Eagle would take the gifts to the mother, grandmother and aunt of Little Flower's mother. He planned to gather the materials needed to build the huti that would belong to Little Flower and to help her plant the corn and beans that would fill their pot. When this was done, he would go on the hunt and bring back the deer for her to skin, the meat for food and the hide to be used in so many ways. This was the way of the Hillabee people; they would then be husband and wife.

Little Flower smiled, thinking of the words Soaring Eagle had said. Seeing the radiant look on her daughter's face, Sunflower Woman could almost guess her thoughts as she spoke. "My daughter looks as pretty as the little flowers popping up in the meadow this day. Would she like to share this happiness with her mother?"

Little Flower, knowing that she had received her name

from the little flowers growing in the meadow, enjoyed her mother referring to those flowers. "Of course, my mother, before the sun is high in the sky on this day, you will receive a visit from Soaring Eagle," and smiling broadly, Little Flower continued, "he will bring gifts for you and grandmother. I will need your help to complete the dress of deer skin that I will wear on the day of celebration."

"Oh my daughter," Sunflower Woman said, as she hugged her daughter to her. "This makes me so happy. How soon will you need the dress to be finished?"

"Soaring Eagle will have the huti built and the corn planted in a few suns. He and my brother then plan to go on the hunt after that is done. We think the day after the next full moon will be the day of celebration for us and for Brave Hawk and Spotted Fawn," Little Flower said excitedly.

"So soon," Sunflower Woman asked as she realized that in only a short time her daughter would be a woman on her own and no longer dependent on her mother.

"Yes, my mother and as quickly as we finish our morning work, we will go to the huti of Spotted Fawn to talk with her mother. Brave Hawk has already talked with the mother and grandmother of Spotted Fawn. He, like Soaring Eagle, wants the plans of marriage to be done in the Creek way. He will follow us with the gifts for them." Little Flower's words quickly came as she tried to contain her excitement, "And after we talk with the mother of Fawn, you and grandmother will receive your visit from Soaring Eagle."

"My Little Flower," Sunflower Woman said. "I am so happy for you and your brother. We have much work to do in preparation for the day of celebration. How is it that the two of you decided to have the same celebration day? Does that not worry you to share that day," she asked, hoping this was what her daughter really wanted.

"The four of us have talked of this, mother, and we all want our wedding celebration to be together. Fawn and I have been the closest of friends all of our lives and Brave Hawk and Soaring Eagle are more like brothers than friends," Little Flower said as she began braiding her beautiful hair. "My brother and my soon-to-be husband both say they will share their lives and that when it is time, they will together make the journey to the place of the Great Spirit. Come mother, this is an important day and we have much to do," Little Flower said, having no way of knowing the prophetic meaning of her words.

Chapter Eight

The next several days passed rapidly. Two new huti were constructed in the Hillabee village, one belonging to Little Flower near that of her mother in the clan of the Wind section, and the other in the Deer Clan area of which Spotted Fawn was a part. Trees had been cleared and corn and beans had been planted. Mothers and grandmothers had been presented with gifts and Soaring Eagle and Brave Hawk had returned from the hunt, each laden with fresh meat to provide for their wives. All had been done just as the Creek way required. No other ritual ceremony was needed for the marriage to be complete. Creek culture did allow the time before the poskeeta ceremony as a trial period in which a man could leave if he so desired. Neither of the new husbands would have any need to leave their wives and both were eager for the day of celebration to begin.

Bright sunlight danced through the trees surrounding the Hillabee village as everyone readied for the marriage celebration. After many days of planning and much preparation, the Hillabee people were excited and greatly anticipated the day. People from all of the Hillabee villages and other surrounding towns including Oafuskee were converging on the square ground. Bountiful supplies of food, deer, turkey, fish, and bread made from dried corn and sofkee flavored with honey had been prepared. As he always did for celebrations, trader Grierson had brought his strong drink of firewater. Again, the men and young warriors had been warned against the evil of consuming too much. Many had proclaimed they would not drink any of the firewater on this day, this in honor of their friends Soaring Eagle and Brave Hawk who were known for never taking the drink.

Little Flower and Spotted Fawn were in the huti of Sunflower Woman and would remain there until the village crier announced their arrival in the square ground by the signal of his flute. Both had spent much time preparing their dresses made of deerskin which had been worked until it was soft and white. Little Flower had sewed the white beads she had earned by working for Sinnugee Grierson onto her dress and also on her matching moccasins.

The young women were strikingly beautiful, both with their hair in long braids and their brown eyes danced with excitement and happiness. Little Flower had become fidgety and impatient and was obviously ready for the celebration to begin. "My mother, when will we hear the sound of the flute? My stomach has the butterflies flying around again."

"Mine has birds chasing the butterflies," Spotted Fawn chimed in.

Sunflower Woman laughed at the two young women, but she too was ready for the day to begin. "Very soon my daughters," she said, already proclaiming Spotted Fawn as her daughter. Just as she leaned to hug both girls, the sweet sound of the flute could be heard. "Little Flower and Spotted Fawn, this is the time of a new life for you, a new beginning and I pray to the Great Spirit that your lives will be happy and long."

Sunflower Woman and the mother of Spotted Fawn each took the hand of their daughter and left the huti. Tears threatened to fall from Little Flower's eyes as she took one last look at the place she had lived all of her life, but the firm grip of her mother's hand reminded her of what was to come.

Seeing the multitude of people lining the square ground, Little Flower thought that surely everyone in every village was in attendance. This was an important day for the Hillabee people and many had traveled far for the celebration. They all enjoyed the dancing, the food and the social involvement with people from villages other than their own. Men talked about the new treaties and encroachment of white men who had broken the treaties. The women caught up on the latest gossip, the maidens flirted openly with the young warriors and the children squealed in delight as they ran and played.

It was a good day for the Hillabee and their friends, one they would long remember. As was the tradition for all ceremonies and celebrations, the Hillabee micco would need to began with words of congratulations to the newly married couple or in this case, couples. The single drum beat indicated for everyone to be silent. The tall muscular man, dressed in his best, the red beads and silver arm bracelets shinning brightly in the sun, stood and quietly surveyed the scene in front of him. He smiled as he slowly turned to see his full audience. "My people and my friends, it is good to see you here on this day of celebration. Some of you may have been here and remember the time of the owls." As he spoke of the time of the owls many nodded their heads. "On that day we celebrated and thanked the Great Spirit for saving the lives of some of our young people. On this day we celebrate again with those same young people." Turning to look at the two couples standing to his left he continued. "Soaring Eagle and Little Flower, Brave Hawk and Spotted Fawn, will you please step forward?" Taking the hand of Little Flower, Soaring Eagle led the way, the other couple followed. "My people of the Hillabee and our friends from other villages please join me today in honoring and congratulating these young people as they begin their new lives together."

    As if some signal had been given, the loud sound of the drums from all around the square ground filled the air. The village people began cheering and keening. Little Flower and Spotted Fawn had not expected the response and were a little embarrassed. Both were more so when their new husbands picked up his wife and began swinging her around and kissing her as if no one watched. This only brought more cheers and whistles from the unmarried warriors. When finally the drums stopped, silence again prevailed. "I see my people are now ready to join in the fun and you may do so in only a short time." Groans were heard from the audience, some of the young people fearing that a long speech was forthcoming. Understanding completely, the micco only laughed, as he too was in the mood for celebrating. "First I must say a few more words. I ask today for the Great Spirit to give Soaring Eagle and his wife Little Flower and Brave Hawk and his wife Spotted Fawn a long, happy life and bless them with many children to carry on the Hillabee way. I ask the Great Spirit to protect them as well as all of the Muscogee people gathered here for this day of celebration. I ask the Great Spirit to make us all strong as we face the troubling times ahead." He paused, wishing for the words he had said to be understood by his people. "I invite each of you now to go and eat. We have much food we wish to share. When stomachs are full we will dance. Soaring Eagle and Brave Hawk will have the first dance with their new wives, then the women may dance and the men may join them. I wish for each of our visitors to enjoy their stay in the town of the Hillabee and may the Great Spirit guide you safely back to your homes." With that the micco melted into the crowd of his people and the festivities began.

The eating and dancing continued long after the last rays of the setting sun had dipped into the horizon. Even after the visitors from the other villages had left to start their trip back to their home, the Hillabee people were not ready for their celebration to end.

Soaring Eagle, looking at this wife, knew she was exhausted and he was tired as well. Not seeing Brave Hawk and Spotted Fawn, he guessed they had already left. "My Little Flower, I think we can let the celebration continue without us. Come; let us go to your huti." The two walked from the square ground hand in hand, neither seeing or caring that the Hillabee people smiled as they saw them go.

As the moon began to rise over the Hillabee Village, no one was aware of another visitor, an uninvited and unwanted one. The owl had secretly entered and was watching and waiting. His time would again come and his presence would be known.

Part Three
Hillabee Town
Time of the Falling Leaves, 1811

Chapter One

Changing and troubling times had not dampened the happiness and spirit of the people of the Hillabee during the five seasons since the big celebration. Other ceremonies and marriages had been celebrated. Babies were born and some of the old ones had gone to be with the Great Spirit.

Soaring Eagle and Little Flower as well as Brave Hawk and Spotted Fawn had settled happily into their new lives. Both warriors had become micco apotka, assistant chiefs, during the poskeeta following their marriage. Many in the village considered them to be the future leaders of the Hillabee and both were well respected. Spotted Fawn had given birth to a son in the next season of new leaves. Little Flower's baby came too soon and was unable to survive the cold season. With heavy hearts she and Soaring Eagle's love grew even stronger and during the next season of falling leaves Little Flower became the mother of two, a strong son and tiny daughter with the fighting spirit and strength of the Hillabee, who would grow into a beautiful little girl.

Many of the Hillabee continued to accept the ways of the white while many others stood firm and refused any more change. Treaties were still made between the so-called "white fathers" and their "red children" and the treaties were still being broken. More white men hunted for food to feed their families on traditional Creek hunting land, leaving less for the Creek. These same white men, living too close to the Creek territory, allowed their cattle and hogs to roam free, destroying the fields of corn the Creek women had planted.

Within the Hillabee village, the gap had widened between those who had accepted the white way and those who had not.

Many stood in the middle, realizing that not everything the whites had introduced to them was bad and, after all, this did make life easier. At the same time, the group with this mindset continued to practice the traditional way and refused to be totally drawn into the beliefs of the others. A balance was maintained within the Hillabee town with all three opinions being tolerated and very little friction occurred. In other down-river towns, the different opinions of the people did cause problems and the gap widened. Agent Benjamin Hawkins, a good man, but one with a governmental job to do, had influenced many people of the Tuckabatchee town. Word had come from the town that a national council would be held there and miccos and warriors from many tribes would gather. It was said that Agent Hawkins was to talk about his government's intention to increase the size of the horse path that ran near Tuckabatchee. It was also said, and there was much excitement about these words, that an important Shawnee leader would attend the council. Upon hearing this news, the Hillabee micco had sent the town crier out to call the people to the square ground.

Being involved in their daily activities, and having no previous warning regarding the micco's talk, many of the Hillabee were slow to respond to the crier's call. When everyone did arrive, the micco wasted no time in beginning his words. "My people of the Hillabee, thank you for coming to hear my words this day. I have heard from our friends from the Tuckabatchee town and there is much excitement there. We have heard already of the disturbing news about the horse path and now word comes that the Shawnee leader, Tecumseh, will arrive soon." Many of the warriors began talking among themselves at the mention of the famed leader's name. Holding up his large hand to silence his warriors, the micco continued, "The big council with the people from many nations attending will begin in four suns. I need for all of the seasoned warriors to make the trip down the Tallapoosa with me. The young warriors and older men will stay here in the village with our women and children. We will leave for Tuckabatchee with the next sun."

Chapter Two

When the Hillabee delegation arrived at the bustling town of Tuckabatchee, they were astonished. Never before had they witnessed as many of their people gathered in one place. Thousands of Creek from all over the confederacy, as well as representatives from other tribes, scouts, traders and white men had all converged to hear the talk of the Shawnee, Tecumseh.

Speculation ran rampant. What would this man, who because of his Creek kinship considered himself a man of the Tallapoosa, have to say? What would his words be to these people who eagerly awaited his talk?

The much anticipated visitor had yet to arrive and the Hillabee group along with the others attending were told by chief Big Warrior to go to the square ground as Agent Benjamin Hawkins was preparing to talk.

Head civil chief Big Warrior, whose face was marked with strange spots, was quite imposing in size and statue. He was much respected by his Creek people even though many said his blood was mixed with those from the north. He had worked well with Agent Hawkins and many of the Tuckabatchee, including himself, had accepted and benefited from the civilization plan.

Big Warrior's closest confidants and those who knew him best also knew that he was not being perfectly honest in regard to his opinion of the whites and their plan of civilization. He watched and listened closely, not completely trusting or believing their words.

Appearing slightly arrogant to some, Big Warrior introduced Benjamin Hawkins to the many of the vast sea of red men who would patiently hear the words of the agent. Most present had heard of him and his plan of civilization and many had heard his talk before but there were others who had not. Some cringed at his opening remark. "My red brothers, I come here today to tell you the good news about the big, new road your white father in Washington is going to build for you."

A few of the more progressive men nodded in agreement but most had the stern look of disapproval on their faces. One of the visiting miccos voiced his thoughts by saying, "This man is not my brother, I have no white father and I do not want any road."

Agent Hawkins, seeing the dark negative looks from some of his audience, continued, "This new road, which is really just the enlarging of the old horse path, will bring great opportunity for the Creek. Stands can be built along the road and ferries can be constructed to cross the river and streams. These can be owned and operated by the Creek people. Much money can be made from the great influx of white families traveling through your land on the way to settlements in the west." Hawkins continued with his long talk. The more he said, the darker the scowls appeared on the faces of this now agitated audience.

When the talk was finished, Big Warrior stood and addressed the large contingent of his people. "My Creek brothers and I will discuss the words Agent Hawkins has spoken. I ask now for our visitors from other nations and Mr. Hawkins to leave our square ground.

In only a short time, Big Warrior had his answer from the miccos and warriors from other towns. The vote was almost unanimous. The Creek did not want the horse path enlarged nor did they want any other road construction near their land. Their answer was final and no further negotiations were necessary. Upon hearing this response from Big Warrior, Agent Hawkins, red-faced and more than a little agitated himself, stood before the Creek, "My brothers and friends…"

Before he could say more a warrior from near the back of the crowd yelled out, "Hawkins, you are not my brother and are no longer my friend." Many around him agreed.

More agitated now, Agent Hawkins again begin to speak, "Your white father in Washington has made his decision. You have no say in the matter. The horse path will be made larger, much larger and it will be called The Federal Road. Many white families will travel the road. My advice to you is to accept this road and make the best of this situation." Hawkins left the square ground amidst loud clamor and disapproval.

Chapter Three

All of the Creek attending the grand council were distraught after hearing the words from Agent Hawkins. What did he mean by saying they did not have a choice? This was the land of the Creek. It did not belong to the great white father. Moods were bad and spirits low when the word was received that Tecumseh was near and would soon arrive in Tuckabatchee. The mood then changed to one of excitement as the multitude of Creek and their neighbors returned to the square ground.

The routine single beat of the drum signaled the entrance of the Shawnee and his entourage into the town. His group included several Shawnee, a few from unknown tribes, and two or three Creek, one of which was Seekaboo, who had family in Tuckabatchee. The sight was breath-taking to the most seasoned warriors. The group was dressed only in breech cloths and moccasins. Silver ornaments adorned their arms, eagle feathers protruded from their long hair and their faces were painted black. Their leader was tall and muscular, his only imperfection, a slight limp. He walked around the square several times and presented the chiefs with a gift of tobacco along with his greetings.

Many stories would be told for generations about Tecumseh and his grand entrance to Tuckabatchee town. The entrance was all there would be on that day as the sun was sinking low in the sky and the northern visitors were escorted to their huts.

The next nine days were a whirlwind of activity around Tuckabatchee town. Family and friends visited, games of chunky were played, and warriors tested each other in various skills of strength. The Dance of the Lakes was taught to the Creek by Seekaboo and many long speeches were made by miccos and beloved men. None of the speeches made were by Tecumseh. All present eagerly anticipated hearing the words of the famed Shawnee. Strangely, each new day brought a different reason as to why the talk would not be given. The sun was too high one day and the next the sun was too low. It soon became apparent that Tecumseh was playing some sort of game or that he was waiting for some unknown reason.

Finally, word was heard from the Shawnee leader that he would not give his talk until Hawkins and all white men had left the town. Becoming tired of playing the waiting game, Hawkins agreed to take his leave from Tuckabatchee. The traders and other whites present also agreed to leave as well. It would be revealed later that one white man, Sam Dale, a scout and trader who had spent much time among the Creek, left but returned to hear the words that would determine the future of the Creek people.

Chapter Four

The final day of September in the year of 1811 was bright and sunny. The waters of the Tallapoosa sparkled in the sunlight. The wind blew soft and the sweet scents of the season of falling leaves filled the air. This was the day the Shawnee leader would speak and the hundreds, even thousands, of the Creek and their neighbors from other tribes would converge near the giant oak tree, known as the Council Oak, under which so many talks in the past had been made.

When the sun was directly overhead the crowd had become so quiet and still, the sound from the great up-river falls could be heard rushing over the huge rocks that filled the river. Then the drum beat signified that the much anticipated event was to begin. A lone figure appeared first, followed by the group that had accompanied him on the day of their arrival. Again, the clothing was sparse; their painted faces gleamed in the sunlight. To some they looked like devils, their demeanor dark and forbidding. Tecumseh walked around the council square sprinkling the ground with tobacco and then threw what remained into the ceremonial fire. He then gave a loud war whoop and stood before Big Warrior and the other miccos from the visiting tribes.

Looking defiant and seemingly filled with a supernatural glow, he began to slowly speak. "My Muscogee brothers, I have come to the home of my ancestors. My mother was born on the banks of this mighty river. I still have family among you." Tecumseh stopped speaking and slowly looked at his audience, each one feeling as if the dark, stern eyes were looking directly at them. "I come to talk with you this day about the future of our people. I want you to understand what the civilization of the white man has done and is doing to us."

The sun was low in the sky before Tecumseh finished his talk. His words were strong and powerful as he emotionally reached out to his Creek brethren. He talked of the white man's broken promises and how they continued to take the home land away from the red race. He talked of how some of their members were so few, those tribes had completely vanished. The impressive warrior told of how so many of their people who made their home all over the land no longer lived as the grandfathers had. He talked of the fight that was to come if the red men were to survive. In a softer tone, he told of his belief in the Great Spirit, the Giver of Breath and how his blessings were bestowed on the red people. He then asked for the warriors to join with him in his plan to unite all tribes together.

Tecumseh finished his speech by implying that all who would not join with him in his stand against the white man were cowards. This did not sit well with many who had heard the talk. The Ridge of the Cherokee said his people were at peace with the whites and would not join Tecumseh.

Big Warrior, who was seen hoisting his tomahawk in the air several times during the speech, declined to join with Tecumseh as well. "Tecumseh my brother," Big Warrior said in his loud stately voice, "I understand the love you have for this land. I also agree with you in regard to our people keeping this land." Big Warrior paused, searching the crowd for those who were in agreement with him, "but the white men here are not our enemy and Agent Hawkins has helped our people to learn new ways from which we have benefited."

"The new ways have made you white and weak. If you continue on this path the mighty Creek Nation will perish," Tecumseh said as he turned and left the square ground. Many who had heard the speech sat in silence while many more rallied with the Shawnee leader, their war whoops filling the air.

Chapter Five

Tuckabatchee Town was in a whirlwind of excitement. Most of those who called the town home agreed with Big Warrior. Some had noticed his actions during the speech, others had understood. Tuckabatchee was a peace town but there were pockets of Red Sticks, those warriors who were ready to join with Tecumseh and fight if necessary to preserve their home. The across-the-river town of Talisi, on the other hand, was running over with the Red Stick faction.

Tecumseh and his followers stayed in the Tuckabatchee area for nearly a month. The plan was to win over and incite more warriors to the red point of view. Seebeego continued to teach the now eager Creek the Dance of the Lakes.

When the appointed time came for him to leave, Tecumseh again spoke with Big Warrior and the remaining micco and warriors from the visiting towns.

"My Creek brothers," Tecumseh begin, his voice strong but showing no anger. "I am disappointed with the reception I have received in the town of my mother. I am sorry to see that so many of the Creek people have accepted the white civilization and have lost the way of the grandfathers." He continued to talk, noting the reaction from a few warriors standing near the edge of the crowd. "I know that you Big Warrior, and many of your friends do not believe me or in me. I speak the truth when I again say that if the Creek people do not stand with me against the tide of the white race, soon you no longer will be able to call this land your home." Becoming more agitated, he continued, "I will take my leave now from the town of Tuckabatchee. When the sun no longer shines on this day and darkness fills the sky, a great light will be seen from horizon to horizon. This will be a sign from the Great Spirit." Pausing for the effect of his words, Tecumseh saw the startled look on the faces of his audience. This was good, he had their full attention. He had heard from some of his British friends that a great comet which had already been seen in England would appear in the southern sky around this time. He was confident that the comet would be bright this night as he had seen the beginning of its light. Now for his closing statement to these foolish people who refused to listen to his warning, he stood tall and confident as his voice became loud and clear for all to hear. "And when I return to my home in the north, I will stomp my foot and every house in Tuckabatchee will fall to the ground. Then you will know and you," pointing his finger at Big Warrior, "will believe."

With that said Tecumseh turned and left the Tuckabatchee square grounds, pleased to see several more of the previously undecided warriors now follow him.

Chapter Six

The congregation of Hillabee had heard the first talk of Tecumseh and had then returned to their upriver home. Only taking two days of travel to reach Tuckabatchee Town, most of the group had made the trip back to hear his closing statement as he prepared to leave the Creek Nation.

The Hillabee, as well as most of the other Creek, were divided on which position was best for them. While most of Tuckabatchee Town had accepted the white civilization, fewer at the Hillabee towns had. More still preferred the traditional way or at least a combination of the two. A position would need to be taken. This was the topic of discussion as the pipe was passed around to the miccos and beloved men on their first night back in Hillabee Town.

"What is your true opinion of the event we have witnessed, Soaring Eagle," the Hillabee micco asked as he passed the pipe on to the beloved man sitting next to him. "What do you think of this man Tecumseh?"

Soaring Eagle, completely comfortable in his position as an assistant micco, answered slowly. "We have known for many seasons that accepting the trinkets and iron axe of the white man would eventually cause trouble for us. We have watched as more and more white families have moved close to the home of the Creek. We have heard of the treaties they have demanded and then have not honored. We knew the day would come. We have talked much about this, now a position must to be taken."

"It sounds like you have decided to join with Tecumseh." One of the high ranking warriors who already considered himself a Red Stick said, interrupting Soaring Eagle.

"No, I have not." Soaring Eagle said continuing with his answer. "The opinion of this council has been, even when I was barely more than a boy that we should watch and listen and be ready. We all heard the words of Tecumseh. He urged the Creek to stand together against the white man and when the time comes, to fight these people if necessary. I do not believe his intentions are for us to take up our bow and arrows yet. We are not ready and we will need the weapons of the white man if we are to succeed. I think our position, for now, is to continue to watch and wait and be ready," Soaring Eagle said as he sat down to allow others to speak.

Another warrior, one of the more progressive in the Hillabee Town, who had accumulated wealth because he had accepted the white way, stood and addressed the group. "What of the words of the man called Dale? Did he not say that Tecumseh said we should kill the white race, even their women and children? How would we benefit by doing this thing? Many of the Creek have prospered from the civilization plan and there is not a man here who does not have an easier life because of things we have acquired from them." Pausing, he looked directly at Soaring Eagle, "and you have just said that the Creek need the weapons of the white man. Do you wish to kill the whites with their own weapons?

The Hillabee micco stood again and looked at the group of miccos and warriors, seeing the division that was beginning to form between them. He realized that it was his responsibility to calm that division.

"What you have said is true. All of us have accepted the white way to some extent, but we also need to preserve the way of our people. I agree with Soaring Eagle. We should watch and wait for now and prepare for the future. As for the words of the white man, Sam Dale, I do not recall hearing Tecumseh say we should kill the women and children of the white race. I think Dale did not understand the Shawnee tongue or else his plan is to create more trouble between the white people and the Creek. I think now we should all go to our huti. We should rest and think about what we have seen and heard. We should think about the words of Tecumseh and what the future will be for our people if we join with him or if we continue to go the way of the white man."

The diplomatic micco bid the Hillabee men a good night.

As the group left the square ground, a few of them heard the distant cry of the owl.

After a few weeks had passed and the required time for Tecumseh and his followers to return home, the Hillabeee people were awakened from their sleep early one morning. Their huti began to move and shake as the ground trembled beneath them. The Hillabee and all the Creek people knew that Tecumseh had indeed returned to his home and he had stomped his foot, just as he said he would.

Chapter Seven

The days and weeks following the visit of Tecumseh to Tuckabatchee had left the Creek people in a state of unrest and confusion. The night the earth moved and the ground shook did nothing to restore calm. Many would continue to follow the white path of civilization, believing that Tecumseh was seeking power for himself and only creating problems for the Creek people. Nor did they believe he had anything to do with the violent tremors that rocked Tuckabatchee and the Creek Nation.

Some enjoyed the easier life the ways of the white race had brought them, but also feared the loss of the land to those same whites. Finally, there were the others, the ever growing group that understood and realized the real danger; they were ready to fight to defend their way of life. These were the Red Sticks.

Each new day brought word of more and more activity from the Red Sticks along the Tallapoosa. Many of the Upper Creek living on the river were a part of the faction. The Lower Creek living on the Chattahoochee River had accepted more of the white way and did not have the same problems as the upper people.

The division between the red and white factions continued to grow and even the children realized something was different. The eight year old twins of Soaring Eagle and Little Flower, Red Fox and Little Deer, had grown into inquisitive and bright children. They were the only children as two more had come before their time was ready and neither would survive. Soaring Eagle and Little Flower were happy as were most of the Hillabee people in spite of the growing tension. Their daily life had returned to as normal as possible. A few weeks after the earth had moved, when Tecumseh had supposedly stomped his foot, Little Flower was preparing the morning meal for her family. Her son ran up to the huti, his sister close behind. "My mother, my mother," the little boy said excitedly. "Are we Red Sticks?"

Little Deer, never being outdone by her brother, quickly asked the second part of the question. "We are not like the white people are we?"

Laughing at her daughter's confusion, Little Flower said, "No, my daughter, we are definitely not like the white people. I think you mean, are we peaceful?"

Being inpatient for the answer, Red Fox, taking the bowl of steaming sofkee from his mother loudly said, "Swift Wolf said his father is a Red Stick and if his father is one, then so is my father."

Not being surprised that her brother would say that he was a Red Stick, Little Flower was not sure how to correctly answer her son. "I think Red Fox, that you should ask your father that question. As soon as he returns from the deer hunt we will both ask him."

"I think mother, that I will be a Red Stick." Slinging his little bow from his shoulder, Red Fox proudly said, "and I will kill every white man I see."

"Me too, me too," Little Deer said as both children ran around the packed clay area in front of their huti.

"Oh no," Little Flower said looking up to see Sunflower Woman walking to the huti. "My mother, did you hear the words of my children? They asked if we are Red Sticks. What do I tell them?"

"Good morning, my daughter. Yes, I did hear my grandchildren. The same question is being asked all around the town. While they do not understand what is happening, they are being affected and they are frightened." Sunflower Woman said smiling. "At least some of them … my grandson and his sister," both women laughed, thinking about Red Fox and his bow, "are ready to take their bow and arrows and fight." Quickly sobering, she continued, "My daughter, I too have much fear for us."

Chapter Eight

The season of cold after the visit of Tecumseh quickly turned into the time of the new leaves. The people of the Hillabee planted their crops of corn and beans, the women making every effort to maintain a calm balance in their lives and that of their family. Each day word came from somewhere in the Creek territory of yet another intrusion by some white man and his family. The mood was becoming dark and angry, the red faction becoming stronger. Friction between those willing to fight and die for their way of life and those who had accepted the white way continued to grow but both sides were determined to keep their homes and what the white man wanted most, the land.

This feeling of discontent and unrest continued into the next warm season. The beloved men warned of the trouble that was sure to come. They predicted that red brothers would fight and kill each other because of the curse of the white man.

The responsibility of Soaring Eagle and Brave Hawk had increased tremendously. Even the Hillabee were caught up in the discord that seemed to be ravaging the entire Creek Nation. Warriors traveling through Hillabee town told of the Red Sticks who planned to kill the old chiefs and burn the white peace villages.

The Hillabee miccos, beloved men and warriors slowly passed their pipe as the sun was sinking behind the old white oak trees that bordered the village. A strange, still, quiet had settled over the group, each one deep in thought as to what words, if any, could be said that would bring peace and happiness again to their people. All of them realized the problems they faced were likely not soluable.

Passing the pipe along to the beloved man that sat beside him, the Hillabee micco with a sad, forlorn expression covering his face, quietly began to speak. "My brothers, my friends, you have heard me say for many seasons now that we should watch and listen and wait." He paused, looking at each of his men eye to eye before he continued, "And be ready. I think that we have waited long enough and on this night we will decide which side we shall take. We will no longer straddle the fence of the white man."

Whoops of agreement were heard coming from the group of Hillabee warriors, all of them realizing what words their micco would say. "The other micco and I have already talked of this before we came to speak you. We know that some of you will not agree with us on this important decision and that is why, in the way of the Creek, we will allow you to have your say. My brothers, with heavy hearts, we the micco of the mother town of the Hillabee say this night we will no longer be influenced by the people of the white race. We will no longer stand by and allow them to take from us our land or our way of life."

More even louder whoops filled the air with only a few men remaining silent. The Hillabee micco knew the response he would receive. He also knew his warriors would be a force to be reckoned with. "Again, I say to my brothers, that any one of you who has a different opinion, may express it. I cannot tell you what to think or what to do."

Two or three warriors near the back of the circle looked at each other. One slowly rose to face the group. "I and my brother here," pointing to the man beside him, "do not wish to fight the white man. It is because of them that we prosper and it is because of them that all Creek people can live an easier life. This is all I have to say."

One of the older warriors stood and calmly remarked. "Yes, we do all enjoy the things the white man has brought to us but we cannot forfeit our homes and our land for iron pots and axes." His voice becoming stronger and louder, he continued, "And I will fight until I can fight no more before I will allow the white man to take my land."

Light from the fire flashed on the faces of the jubilant warriors as all but a few joyously whooped and yelled that they too would fight to the end. This continued on until the moon rose high in the night sky. The micco then bid his people to return to their huti. Again, this time close and loud enough for each warrior to hear, the mournful cry of the owl filled the air.

Chapter Nine

Three suns after the majority of the Hillabee mother town had voted to join with the Red Sticks; the village awoke to sounds of gun fire and loud whoops. Smoke could be seen rising from across White Oak Creek, the area of the Grierson Farm. In complete shock and amazement the Hillabee warriors rushed out of their huti, each grabbing his gun or bow. Running to the bank of the creek, they stared in disbelief at what they witnessed. The farm and factory area of Trader Grierson was under attack, but who were the attackers? One of the warriors nearest the creek noticed a lone figure crossing the bridge which joined the farm and the village. As he hoisted his rifle to his shoulder and prepared to fire, the figure on the bridge loudly called out to the onlookers, "Hold your fire! Do not shoot!"

Lowering his gun, the Hillabee warrior loudly called back to the man who had now reached the village side of the creek. "Who are you and what is going on?"

The warrior, obviously a Red Stick, showed no fear as he addressed the large group of Hillabee men. Some of them began to run toward the bridge to offer assistance to those on the other side. "No, do not go there! This is not your fight, but if you attempt to help," he paused as the clamor from across the creek began to subside, "it will become yours."

The Hillabee warriors stopped and the micco asked again, "Who are you and why has the Grierson property been attacked?"

"I am Bear Killer. My town is Autosse. I was sent to warn you not to interfere in the business of this day. We have heard of your decision to fight with us against the white man. We welcome your help."

The micco, still looking concerned, glanced across the creek, a part of him wanting to help. "But why have the Red Sticks attacked Grierson. What has he done to provoke this? I know some of his people are hurt and may have been killed."

With a look of scorn, the Autosse warrior said as he turned to cross back over the creek, "Grierson and other white men like him are the reason our people are divided. He was not satisfied just to bring the way of the white man into the world of the Creek, he also took our land. His words are against the Red Sticks. He has said that we should not fight against the white man, that we should allow others, as he has done, to take our land and our home." Looking at the Hillabee micco he continued, "When the sun has risen above the trees, you may go and help this man your," he paused, "your friend, but remember you too are a Red Stick and you will spill the blood of the white man just as he will spill yours."

Chapter Ten

The Hillabee micco and his warriors watched as the Red Stick crossed the creek and vanished into the woods that bordered the farm. Realizing that bows were likely drawn and ready to be released if any of them attempted to cross the bridge, they stood and waited for the sun to rise over the tree tops.

The Hillabee warriors had never experienced the agenda of the Red Sticks and some of them were deeply shaken about what had happened. One or two of them began to speak, but were silenced by the micco. "We will talk of this when the time is right. Now, the sun shows over the tops of the trees. We will go help the people who are our friends."

The Hillabee men rushed across the bridge and up the path that led to the Grierson Farm complex. Smoke filled the air from a burning log cabin. Cries for help could be heard from all around the farm. Men, women and children stood dazed, some of them looking at lifeless bodies, unseeing eyes staring back.

Several hours passed before any calm could be restored to the Grierson Farm. Women from the Hillabee Village were sent for to help with the injured and to look after the children. When a complete search of the farm complex had been made, the bodies of twelve were placed in front of the Grierson house. Showing no favor to any of their victims, the marauding Red Stick had killed red, black and white, including a son of Trader Grierson.

Sinuggee Grierson stood in shock as she viewed the scene. The place she had called home for many years had been ransacked and was in shambles. Some of the out buildings still smoldering, her looms and cotton all destroyed. For some reason, known only to the attacking Red Stick, the Grierson home was not torched. Inside the house, all of the furnishings from the white world were broken and scattered as if to relay their message.

A much younger Creek woman wrapped in a blanket came and stood beside Sinuggee. Tears streamed down her brown face as she looked at the body of the brother of her husband. Sinuggee, reaching for a pair of trade scissors, attached to her belt, placed her arm around the woman. Both began the centuries, old keening ritual of mourning. Taking the scissors, the heart-broken mother, slowly cut one of the long braids of her hair. With the keening becoming louder, the second braid fell to the ground. The younger woman did the same.

As the sun moved across the sky, other Hillabee women joined the two. All could share in their sorrow. Seeming to compose herself, Sinuggee looked at the wife of her still-living son, seeing that she was clothed only in a blanket. "Star Woman, why do you have a blanket wrapped around you? Where is your skirt and shirt?"

"Mother Sinuggee," she sobbed. "The Red Stick warriors took my clothes and threw them into the fire."

Anger flashed across the mournful face of the Creek woman. "Were you…did they hurt you?"

"No, mother, I was not touched, only deeply ashamed," Star Woman said, beginning to cry again, "and humiliated."

"Do not cry anymore my daughter. Tears will not change what has happened and it will not bring back those that," Sinuggee visibly stood straighter and taking a deep breath, "have been lost today. It is sad for me to know that my own people would do this. At the same time, I understand and I have known for many seasons that this would one day happen."

Chapter Eleven

The remainder of the day was spent at the Grierson Complex, the Hillabee men burying the dead and salvaging what was left of the vast farm and factory. The Hillabee women were asked to prepare food for the Grierson family and their workers since the Red Sticks had taken all food supplies. A large number of cattle had been slaughtered and the horses were stolen. Making sure the complex was left in total devastation and with no ready way to rebuild; most of the Grierson family's slaves had been taken hostage.

An eerie silence had settled over the complex as the sun began to set behind the white oak trees. The Grierson people had been offered food; few had any desire to eat. The group sat around a central fire in front of the big cabin.

The Hillabee micco and his warriors had spent an exhausting day helping their neighbors and were ready to go to their village and rest. Seeing the sorrow and heartbreak in the face of the man who had been his friend for many seasons, the micco walked over and sat down by Robert Grierson. Foregoing any formality that might have under normal circumstances been used, the Hillabee leader softly said, "My friend, my brother, my heart is filled with sadness for you and your family."

The once vibrant eyes of a prosperous, energetic man had turned into those of a broken man filled with such sorrow that surely his heart was breaking. Robert Grierson looked at the Hillabee for a long moment, no longer able to control the hot tears that streamed down his suddenly aging face. Composing himself, he slowly began to speak. "My friend, my true friend, thank you for your kindness and for the help of your people. I have lived among you for many seasons." His voice breaking again, "It was never my intention to harm any of the Creek people. My trades have always been fair. What has happened is of no fault of the Hillabee people. I should have taken the warning given me. I should have been ready for this attack but I was not and I have lost much, including my son and the people who have worked for me who were like my family. Oh! What have I allowed to happen?" Burying his face in his hands the sorrowful man once again began to cry.

His Creek wife setting by his side placed her strong hand into his. "My husband, do not blame yourself. We have indeed lost much on this day. We will find the strength from deep within to carry on," Sinuggee said as she again began softly keening.

The Hillabee micco gently touched the shoulder of his friend. "We will leave you now. I know that you need time alone. We will return before the sun is high in the sky on the next new day."

The Hillabee warriors left the desolate Grierson Complex and crossed the bridge back into the Hillabee village. As they approached the village, the eerie quite was broken by the chilling sound of the owl. Not only one, but the sound of many filled the air of the twilight evening.

Chapter Twelve

The men were tired and hungry, but each of them without being told, went directly to the square ground. Words must be said about the actions of the day. Words of different opinions would be voiced. The micco requested that water and food be brought to the square ground for his warriors. He slowly lit the pipe he had removed from his belt. Taking a deep breath he looked at his attentive warriors, most of whom he knew would do what he asked. The distant sound of the owl could still be heard as he began to speak. "Brothers," he paused, "my friends, listen. Do you even now hear the cry of the owl?" Each warrior nodded his head. "We have heard his cry for many seasons. Some of our beloved men have said this is a dark, forbidding sign, one that will surely affect all of us. We have experienced on this day the warning of the owl … death and destruction. On this day we saw the wrath of our own people." He again paused, seeing the agreement on the faces of his warriors. "What happened was wrong. Trader Grierson did nothing to deserve this. He has been a good friend to us for many seasons." The micco took a long draw from his pipe, the smoke encircling his head. "I am sorry this has happened but … I also understand."

Some of the warriors made audible sounds of agreement. "Trader Grierson did make statements against the Red Sticks and he has made changes, I do admit, some of them have been good for the Creek people." More words of agreement arose from the group while others remained silent. "We have agreed to fight with the Red Sticks when and if it is necessary and we have also promised to help Trader Grierson restore his farm. I ask now to hear words from those who will assist me and also from my warriors. First, what is the opinion of Soaring Eagle and Brave Hawk?" The micco sat down, fatigue showing in his strong face.

Soaring Eagle stood before the group of his friends and fellow warriors, warriors who would soon endure much pain and sorrow together. "Brothers, I am torn. On this day we have witnessed the death and destruction that some of our people are capable of doing. As our micco has said, this was an unfair deed…or was it? If Trader Grierson was not our friend, if we had not known him for many seasons, would we have done as the Red Stick attackers did on this day?" Soaring Eagle too sat down shaking his head as if he did not know the answer to his own question.

Brave Hawk stood and addressed the group. "In answer to your question Soaring Eagle, yes we would have attacked the Grierson camp. The man may be our friend, but he has also caused harm and trouble for our people. He came long ago to live among us. He tempted our fathers and grandfathers with iron hatchets and weapons of the white man and the mothers of our people with beads and trinkets. He took our land and made it his home and it has continued to grow in size." Brave Hawk's voice grew louder as the warriors around him became more animated. "Now Grierson has said the Red Sticks, that we, have no right to fight for what is ours."

The Hillabee men talked and exchanged views until the moon rose high in the night sky. Many of the opinions were like those of Brave Hawk while others were totally opposed to the Red Stick movement. Still others were like Soaring Eagle and the micco, wanting peace for their people but not willing to give in to any more demands from the white man.

After hearing all who wished to talk, the micco stood and issued one final request. "It is late and we are tired. We should go to our huti and rest. Any of you who wish may come with me to the Grierson Farm when the new sun is over the white oak trees. We will do what we can to help. Please remember this. We have different opinions but the Hillabee are still one people."

Chapter Thirteen

The summer of 1813 was one of unrest among the Creek people living along the Tallapoosa River. The attitude of the people, just as the flow of the river, was turbulent and at times violent. Warriors passing through Hillabee town told of the increasing surge in the Red Stick movement. Threats on the life of the old chiefs and the destruction of peace villages were issued on a daily basis. Never before had the Creek people felt as much animosity for each other. With unsatisfied thirst for more land, the white man and his family continued to edge closer and closer to the Creek boundary.

Depredations had occurred for years, the Creek stealing a cow or horse from a white man's farm, the white man slipping too far into Creek hunting land, killing the deer and taking food from the warrior's family. With tempers short, the inevitable finally happened. White blood was shed by the hand of the red and in retaliation, the Creek must be held accountable. These events continued to escalate and the Creek in all areas of the nation could feel the imminent explosion between the two races in the making. Even the children were aware of the turmoil and uneasiness running rampart in the Creek towns. The children of the Hillabee towns may have been even more so as warriors of different factions traveled along the trade path near the town.

Sitting outside the huti, Little Flower and Sunflower Woman were busy mending the moccasins of the children, their conversation naturally centered on the division among the Hillabee people. "Mother," Little Flower said, "I know you have warned me for a long, long time about the things that are occurring now. Before, in the time of the owl, when I was only a little girl, you said this would happen."

"Yes, my daughter." Sunflower Woman said, apprehension showing in her still beautiful face, "I did. I fear we will have much worse to face. Now, I fear not only the loss of our homes and land, but also …" pausing to brush away the tears that always came when she talked of the future, "I fear for the lives of our people, for the life of your father and of your husband, for you and the children." Sunflower Woman's words were interrupted by the loud shouts from her grandson.

"Mother, my mother, I saw them. I saw them." Red Fox excitedly yelled as he ran to his mother's side.

"Slow down Red Fox." Little Flower said, trying to calm her son. "Who did you see and where is your sister?"

"I saw the Red Stick warriors. They are on the trade path down by White Oak Creek and my father is talking with them."

Knowing that the Red Stick warriors often traveled the path, Little Flower was not too concerned until her son said they were talking to Soaring Eagle and she still did not know where Little Deer was.

"Talking with your father?" Little Flower asked, "and again, my son, I ask where is your sister, concern showing on her face.

"Mother, I do not know where Little Deer is. She was with me on the path before we hid behind the big rock when we saw the Red Sticks coming."

Before Little Flower could speak again she saw her husband. With him were several warriors, the wind blowing the red feathers in their hair. As they walked into the village, Little Flower saw that one was holding the hand of Little Deer, the child smiling broadly up at the warrior.

Realizing the visiting warriors meant no harm; Little Flower remained calm and waited for an explanation from her husband.

"Little Flower, our daughter has decided that instead of becoming a beautiful Creek maiden, like her mother," Soaring Eagle smiled at his wife, "that she will be a Red Stick warrior." The warriors laughed at the remark and Little Deer was returned to her mother. "She and her brother were hiding behind the big rock on the path and it seems," looking at his wide eyed son, Soaring Eagle continued, "that her brother decided to leave without his sister. These are my friends from Talisi town and they are hungry after their travel up river. Would you bring them some sofkee and some parched corn and they will continue on their way."

"Yes, my husband, come children, you can help me," Little Flower said, taking the hand of each child.

The warriors ate the food offered to them and filled their pouches with dried corn. After a few more words to Soaring Eagle the warriors left the Hillabee village, the new friend of Little Deer taking the time to pat the head of each child as he walked by them. Turning to look at his host, the handsome Red Stick warrior said, "The children are the reason."

Soaring Eagle and his family watched as the group of Red Stick warriors made their way up the path, not looking like the savages they were accused of being. Breaking the silence, Little Flower said to her husband, "I did not know you had friends at Talisi town."

"Yes, they are my friends." Soaring Eagle said, "The tall one who has shown kindness to our children is known as McQueen. They are making plans to soon travel to a town called Pensacola to meet with men who will provide us with lead and powder for our guns."

Chapter Fourteen

Garnering more support for the Red Stick cause, the warriors had traveled to the upper areas of the Creek Nation. They were indeed a part of the large group who traveled to the Spanish controlled town of Pensacola. Some of the warriors, after partaking of the white man's firewater, had taken their mischief too far. En-route to their destination, the warriors paid a visit to the farm of a hapless Mr. Cornells. Mr. Cornells was part Creek himself and was not at home when his guest arrived.

Returning home, he found the smoking remains of his farm house. His wife and a man that had been visiting with them had been taken hostage. Mrs. Cornells would later be traded for a blanket. Some of the sober and less hot-headed of the group had cautioned against this action. "We will regret the deed that has been done here on this day." One of the Creek visitors said as they left the scene of their senseless act.

"Yes," another said, "Now we will need to contend with this irrational woman and this sorry excuse for a man. If all white men were like this one we could have them all running like camp dogs."

"More importantly, we have alerted the white people that we are on the move and they will know where we are going. I am sure by now the reason for our trip is known. We must use caution," another warrior said.

The group continued their journey and in two suns they entered the bustling frontier town of Pensacola. The group under the leadership of Peter McQueen met with the Spanish governor. The governor was not particularly interested in providing any lead and powder, much less the amount requested. The group of red warriors only received another meeting time. Not happy with the arrangement, McQueen did urge his men to avoid any mischief. Upon meeting with the governor a second time, a token amount of powder and lead was secured.

Being extremely disappointed in the amount of ammunition received, McQueen reminded the governor of the many Creek towns containing thousands of warriors ready to fight when the time came. "I know your intentions are to pacify me and to send us on our way with so little powder. Our intention, Sir," using the white term for respect, McQueen sarcastically continued, "was not to fight the white race. It does appear now, this may have changed. We will be ready."

Before leaving, McQueen and his warriors danced on the cobblestone street, their war chants sounding throughout the town. Two men, one white, the other mixed with the blood of both red and white, standing on the street had been watching the band of warriors and knew their purpose. They would leave just ahead of them and would sound the alert that Red Sticks were coming back with ammunition.

Chapter Fifteen

McQueen and his band of Red Stick warriors had been disappointed in the amount of powder and lead they had received, but nevertheless, several pack horses had been loaded with valuable cargo. Being jubilant about the return trip home, the warriors were careless. While they were resting and eating the midday meal alongside Burnt Corn Creek, they were attacked. The spying men from Pensacola wasted no time in gathering a local group of loosely formed militia. The group, consisting of farmers and friendly Creek with loaded muskets, had the upper hand on the unsuspecting Red Sticks.

Recovering from the surprise attack, the Red Stick warriors returned fire for a short time and then retreated into the swamp. McQueen rallied his men and converged on a divided militia. While part of the militia was fighting, others caught the pack horses. The momentum changed and soon the attackers were retreating in confusion and fear.

The Red Stick force returned to the camp site. A dozen of their companions had been killed and the horses loaded with the much needed lead and powder had been taken. Realizing the attack could have been avoided if guards had been posted, Peter McQueen addressed his men. "We were careless and because of that we have lost twelve of our good warriors. We have also lost the lead and powder we will need. If the white people want to fight, we will be ready. This is only the beginning and the death of these men will be avenged. We are now at war with these white people and the Creek who have chosen to assist them."

The Red Stick warriors placed the bodies of the slain warriors on the remaining horses and resumed their journey back to the Tallapoosa. One young warrior said to his friend as they left camp, "We could have killed all of them if we had followed them. They were screaming and crying like a pack of devils was on their trail."

His companion laughed and said, "We are not devils, but if we had caught them it would have been hell for them." Little did the two young warriors know what the future would hold for them and the Creek Nation. As their leader had said, this was only the beginning.

Chapter Sixteen

Word traveled rapidly from village to village and the Hillabee people soon learned of the attack on the warriors at Burnt Corn Creek. None of the Hillabee warriors had traveled with them, but many did have friends and relatives among the group. The talk at the square ground between the Hillabee warriors reflected their divided opinions. Some cried for revenge of the slain warriors, while others blamed the Red Sticks who had committed the deed at the Cornell farm.

A warrior, who preferred peace rather than fighting, asked the question, "Why did McQueen allow his warriors to commit this act? Surely, he knew the Creek, all of us, would be held responsible."

Soaring Eagle, always thinking and responding with reason was quick to answer. "We know ourselves what effect the firewater of the white man can have and some of our people are not thinking clearly now. Remembering this, Peter McQueen is a good leader and he will do what he thinks is best for his people. This is a bad time for us and we will need to stand together or else we shall all perish."

The Hillabee micco agreed with his assistant and greatly respected friend. "Soaring Eagle is right. We must stand together for strength. If we are divided, we will become weak. I know some of our people do not agree with this. For the sake of the Hillabee people, we will be united and we will be strong."

In spite of the motivating words spoken by the light of the fire, the Hillabee men returned to their huti with heavy hearts. They realized that fighting would result in death and destruction. Regardless of the opinion, whether red or white, fighting and death were imminent, not only for the Hillabee, but for all the Creek people.

Chapter Seventeen

Sunflower Woman wiped the moisture from her cheeks as she finished hoeing the grass from around the corn and bean plants, both of which would provide food in a few suns. She knew many of the towns had planted very little during the season of planting. She also knew many would be hungry because of this. The Hillabee women were determined that their families would have food and they would share with those who were hungry if the need arose. "Grandmother," the small voice of her granddaughter called out. "Can we stop now? I am tired and I would like to eat," Little Deer said, hurrying to catch up with Sunflower Woman.

"Yes, we can stop." Smiling, Sunflower Woman continued, "When you finish hoeing around the corn assigned to you. I think," looking back to count the stalks that had not been weeded, "that you have three more to do."

"Oh, Grandmother, why can I not stop? I have other important things to do." Little Deer smiled sweetly at her grandmother, hoping she would give in to her desire to stop working.

"What is more important than having food to eat when we are hungry, my grand daughter?"

"Yes, Grandmother, I will finish my work," the little girl dejectedly replied.

"I will help you, Little Deer. Why do you not wish to finish your work," Sunflower Woman asked.

"Grandmother, my brother is helping to gather stones for the warriors to make the heads for their arrows. Red Fox said they will need many arrows when the time comes for us to fight. I wish to help gather stones too and I will need more arrows for my bow," Little Deer said as she proudly chopped the last weed from around a corn stalk, aware that her grandmother had helped her finish.

Amused at her granddaughter, but also fearing that she too planned to fight, Sunflower Woman took the long stick with the attached iron blade from the child. "What does your brother think of you helping him?"

"He does not know. I know where the good stones are to be found and he does not. When he tells me to go away," the little girl flashed her sweet smile again, "I will share my stones with him and the warriors will show praise for him, but they will know it was Little Deer who found the stones. They will make the arrowheads and give a few to me."

"What will you do with the arrows Little Deer," Sunflower Woman asked.

"Grandmother, I will fight the white people who try to take our land. If any of our people who live on the river called Flowered Rocks gets in the way, I will fight them too."

Shocked at the words of her granddaughter and wondering where she had gained the information about the Lower Creek living on the Chattahoochee, Sunflower Woman could only say, "you may go Little Deer. First, go to the stream and wash the dirt from your face, and then go to your huti to eat a bowl of sofkee and braid your hair." Laughing at the expression on the child's face, she continued, "You may act like a boy, but you are a girl and you should look like one."

"Yes, Grandmother, I will. Thank you, Grandmother." Turning back to face the aging woman she asked, "Where is my mother? She has not been in our huti since we made our morning meal and she did not tell me what she would do this day."

"I do not know. I will go in search of her. You go now before the sun gets too high in the sky," Sunflower Woman said not showing the concern she felt for her daughter. Bending to pick up her stick hoe, she saw the fleeting movements of a bird as the child walked away from the field. Thinking it to be only a song bird, Sunflower Woman experienced a wave of cold fear wash over her when she heard the distinct cry of the owl.

Chapter Eighteen

Little Flower and Soaring Eagle walked hand and hand along the bank of Cedar Creek. Neither had spoken since Soaring Eagle had found his wife sitting by the big rock staring out at the flower-filled meadow, tears falling from her eyes. He had taken her hand and pulled her gently to him, tenderly brushing away her tears. They walked deep into the woods before sitting down on a large log near a small waterfall that spilled over rocks in the creek. Soaring Eagle spoke first, a young rabbit startled by the voice, scampered away.

"My Little Flower," Soaring Eagle said as he lifted his wife's small hand to his lips. "My flower, please do not cry. I know you are afraid. I too am concerned for us and our people. We must have strength and be brave."

Tears began to fall again from the beautiful eyes of Little Flower as she fell into the arms of her husband. "I am sorry my Eagle. I try not to cry and let my feelings show to others, but I am so afraid. Last night, I dreamed again of our child screaming and I could not help her." She paused, wiping the fresh tears from her eyes. "I also dreamed of the owls. There were many of them and they were so loud." Little Flower covered her ears as if she could stop the cry of the owls. "Eagle, what are we to do? Will we kill or be killed? Will we live to see the children of our children or will we all perish by the hands of the white man?" She paused, "Or by the hand of our own people?"

Soaring Eagle looked long into the eyes of his wife. He realized she was right. Whether they would live or they would die, the decision was not one they could make. I would be made for them.

The two slowly walked back to the village, both deep in their sad thoughts. The silence was broken as the twins were heard yelling in delight at finding their parents. "My mother," Little Deer shouted first, quickly followed by the voice of her brother.

"My father," yelled Red Fox. Both children ran into the open arms of Little Flower and Soaring Eagle.

"Where have you been? We have been looking all around the town for you," Little Deer said as her father lifted her into his arms.

"We have much to tell you," Red Fox said, laughing as his mother pretended to struggle as she picked him up. Not all Creek parents showed as much affection for their children as Soaring Eagle and Little Flower. It was obvious there was much love among the little family.

"What do you need to tell us," Little Flower asked, glad that her tears had stopped falling.

"We have been finding good stones for the warriors to make the heads of their arrows," Little Deer excitedly said.

"And they are going to give us arrows for helping them," Red Fox added.

"What are you going to do with the arrows," Soaring Eagle asked, a knot forming in his stomach.

"We are going to fight the white people," Red Fox proudly said.

"And I am going to help," Little Deer said, "I think, father, my bow needs a new string before we fight." Both children ran ahead of their parents arguing which one would kill the first white man.

Chapter Nineteen

In spite of the talk of war, the Hillabee people valiantly continued to maintain their life as normal during the long days of the hot season. Some of the young, mischievous warriors left the town for several days, returning with injuries inflicted by the ball from the musket of the white man. Others returned with a horse or cow stolen from a farm bordering Creek land. Regardless of this diversion, custom required the annual ritual of the busk ceremony to continue. The elders and beloved men said this ceremony was more important now as the body and mind of the Hillabee and all Creek people needed to be spiritually cleansed.

The four days of busk at the villages of the Hillabee had been one of both celebration and renewal. On the last day, after the fasting and cleansing had been completed, the time of celebration began. The Hillabee people had put thoughts and concern of war away. They ate the new corn and fresh meat and, adorned in new clothing, danced until the moon waned in the night sky. The evening of celebration concluded with the dance of war. The warriors danced with abandon, totally entranced in performing the acts in dance they knew would soon be done in reality. Sweat gleamed on their nearly naked bodies. Knife blades flashed in the dying fire light, some seemed to be in a trance-like state of mind. When near the point of exhaustion, the warriors stopped the dancing.

The Hillabee warriors and their people returned to their huti by the light of the fading moon and the cries of the owl were deafening in the night air. Before the moon would again be full, word came that revenge had been taken for the warriors lost at Burnt Corn. Shock and dread filled the Hillabee micco as the down-river runner had informed him of the actions of the Red Stick warriors. The information was quickly given to the other head men and warriors.

The Hillabee micco stood tall, his strong face showing signs of great concern. "My brothers," he paused for such a length of time that his men began to look from one to the other. Finally, he began again, "My brothers, I called you here to inform you of a deed which took place two suns ago. At the time of the midday meal, the Red Stick warriors, some who were our friends, attacked the stockade at Mims Farm near where the Alabama and Tombigbee waters meet. The Hillabee men sat perfectly still, their attention focused on the words of the micco.

"I was told that after the Burnt Corn incident, soldiers, white families along with their slaves, mixed families and many Creek, who had sided with the whites, went to the stockade for safety," the micco smiled ruefully, "from the Red Sticks. Paying no attention to warnings, the gate was left wide open and the Red Stick warriors," speaking as if the Hillabee were not considered a part of the group, he continued, "under the leadership of Red Eagle and Peter McQueen, killed or maimed all but a very few of the inhabitants. My informant said that more than three-hundred, including women and children, were killed." The micco stopped speaking, a sorrowful look covering his face.

"Red Eagle was a leader?" A warrior asked. "He is a relative of my wife. He has much land and lives as the white. Why would he do this?"

Another warrior added, "He does have more white blood than Creek, but he has much love for the people of his mother."

"I was told that demands were made of Red Eagle to lead and that he tried to prevent much of the killing," the micco answered. "Sadly, there was no stopping the action and all the buildings inside the stockade were torched." The micco paused, seeing the sickening sight in his mind, "Many of the Red Sticks, our people, were also killed."

Another warrior, having strong Red Stick ties, stood, saying, "Why did the white soldiers," he scornfully asked, "not fight back? Why was the gate open? Why did they not take the warning?"

Yet another warrior said, "The white soldiers must be weak

and hid behind the skirts of women." Some of the Hillabee warriors laughed at the remark while others, like their micco, understood the pretentious meaning of the attack.

"This was not wise," Soaring Eagle said. "Now many white soldiers will come to avenge their dead. They will kill our women and our children and burn our villages. This attack is the beginning of a very bad time for our people. I fear how this will end."

Chapter Twenty

The statement made by Soaring Eagle proved to be very prophetic. Within days of the attack of the Mims Farm, the Hillabee knew the fleeting scrimmages which had occurred would now escalate into a full-scale war between the Creek and the white setters and the soldiers that were bound to protect them. This massacre of hundreds of helpless white people, WILL NOT BE TOLERATED, was echoed across the country. Word was soon received that troops from the states of Georgia, Mississippi and Tennessee would converge on the Creek Nation.

One backward soldier from Tennessee was particularly incensed by the Fort Mims Massacre, as the battle was soon called. This brawny, red-headed, short-tempered man had lost his father in a frontier attack by marauding Indians years before. He saw this as the opportunity to avenge his father's death as well as the death of all the white people who were murdered at this place called Mims. This soldier wanted to immediately raise and train troops to make the trip into the Alabama wilderness, but first he would need to recover from wounds received in a duel, the musket ball still lodged in his shoulder. The name of this soldier became familiar and one that was not soon forgotten by the Hillabee or the Creek Nation. His name was Jackson ... Andrew Jackson.

They did not yet know of this soldier as the Hillabee men smoked their pipes and talked of what had happened. Little had been talked of since the word of the massacre had come to them. The mood in the Hillabee town, as in all of the villages and towns, was dark and tense. Many of the people were anxious and some expressed fear of reprisal.

The words of the brother of Little Flower surprised many who sat near the fire. Brave Hawk, normally a man of few words, stood, his tall muscular body silhouetted by the fire light. "My friends, what have our people done? Do they not realize how many white soldiers will now come into our land to fight and kill us? I know we have aligned ourselves with the Red Sticks. I know some of you have joined with them in raids. I also know that it is necessary to protect our homes and our families and fight to defend the land of the Hillabees."

"What are you saying, Brave Hawk," one of the Hillabee who had just returned from a raid asked. "That we not fight for our land. That we allow these white dogs to take what belongs to the Hillabee and the Creek people?"

"No, I am not saying that," Brave Hawk said, realizing he had opened up an argument. "I too will fight when it is the right time. I think we should choose the time and not allow ourselves to be pulled into a battle we cannot win. We should not become involved with the killings of white women and children. We are people of the Hillabee. We do not kill babies, red or white!"

The Hillabee micco stood and raised his hand to silence the warriors before the words turned to anger. "My men of the Hillabee, there will be no quarrel among us. Any of you who wish to fight with the Red Sticks are free to do so. I agree with Brave Hawk that we will choose our battle and when the time is right, we will join the fight. We will defend the home of the Hillabee at any cost."

Chapter Twenty-One

Word of brief skirmishes between the Red Stick warriors and the white soldiers continued to reach the Hillabee. The fighting seemed to be confined to the lower regions of the Tallapoosa and Alabama River as this was the area of the largest Red Stick concentration. As the time of the cold season drew closer and more troops from the State of Tennessee infiltrated the Coosa River Valley, the Hillabee realized the upper river towns were possibly the next targets of the white soldiers.

A great stillness fell over the town as the runner from up river announced the terrible news that the Coosa River town of Tallussahatchee had been attacked. "The white soldier by the name of Coffee and his nine-hundred men has killed every warrior in the town and their numbers were many. All of the women and children have been taken prisoner. We do not know where," the runner said as he tried to catch his breath. "I was told to tell the Hillabee people to prepare, the white army is moving in the direction of the Tallapoosa."

The village was filled by the sorrowful sound of the keening women, some cutting their hair as tears of sorrow ran down their face. The warriors talked quietly among themselves, several taking their pouch and bow, leaving the village in the direction of the north. The owls seemed to encircle the Hillabee town, their cries more sorrowful than the crying women.

The sun had rose and set only six times when the Creek runner again appeared in the Hillabee village. He talked quietly with the Hillabee micco and the cry of aguish from the micco could be heard throughout the village.
Trying to compose himself, the micco called the people to the square ground. He stood motionless as his people came and stood before him. "My people, my Hillabee people," he said as tears formed in his eyes, "I have news from the town of Talladega." Many women instantly began keening; knowing their friends and some family members lived with the Talladega

people. "We have talked of our people becoming divided and even fighting between the peace groups and the red side." He paused as his people waited for his next words. "It seems that some of the hostile warriors have taken the peace town under siege, their only reason being that the Talladega would not join with them. The Talladega micco with the skin from the hog of a white man covering his body slipped out of the town and asked for help from the white troops from Tennessee." Moans of disbelief rose from the warriors as the micco continued. "The big, ugly man who is called Jackson by the whites, with many hundred soldiers came down the Coosa River from the place called Ten Islands. The people of Talladega were freed from the Red Stick warriors," he paused again; waiting for the reaction he knew would come. "It is not known if the peaceful warriors were left at the village or taken prisoner by the white soldiers."

"And the Red Stick warriors, what was their fate?" A painted warrior from the back of the crowd yelled over the murmur of the people. "Was there a battle?"

With an unmistakable tone of sadness, the Hillabee micco continued, "Yes, yes, a battle did ensue. The Red Stick loss was great. "He stopped, clearing the lump in his throat, "As many as four-hundred were slain. There is something else I should tell you. Part, if not the entire town, was burned…along with the warriors. A statement was made by a back woods soldier that the bodies of the Red Sticks who had fallen into a cellar were cooking like potatoes." The micco stopped speaking and a quietness of death settled on the village and the only sound heard came from the owls.

Chapter Twenty-Two

The following day the micco again called his people to the square. "Sadness fills my heart on this day, my people," he said. "Sadness and now fear. The course of the white soldiers from the place called Tennessee will make our village the next to feel their rage for the Creek people. My chiefs and beloved men have talked with Trader Grierson and he has a suggestion he hopes will save our village."

The micco stepped aside as Grierson took his place in front of the Hillabee people. Many looked at him with open contempt as his white peace opinion was well known. "My friends, I join you in your sadness for the Tallussahatchee and Talladega people who were lost. I do not want the Hillabee people to suffer such a fate. I will go and any of the miccos who wish may go with me to Fort Strother on the Coosa. This is the place where the soldier Jackson may be found. I will tell him the Hillabee will not fight against the white soldiers. I will tell him the Hillabee do not support the Red Stick faction, that you only want peace. I will ask that the Hillabee village not be attacked."

"Why do you think Sharp Knife Jackson will listen to you?" The same painted warrior who had raised questions the night before asked. "Are you a friend of this man who kills the women and babies of the Creek people?"

"No, I am not his friend. I repeat, I do not want my Hillabee friends to suffer any harm. This is all I know to do. I have heard that Jackson will pass by peace villages if they make it known to him," Grierson said as he moved aside for the micco, fully aware of the scornful looks he received from some of the painted warriors.

The micco looked to his assistants and beloved men who quickly nodded in approval. "I think Mr. Grierson that some of us will be making the trip up the mighty Coosa to this Fort Strother. We will talk to Sharp Knife Jackson and we will tell him the Hillabee people want no part of his battles."

"You will regret this for as long as you see the sunrise," the painted warrior said as he stalked away, his bow held tightly in his hand.

Grierson, the Hillabee micco, Brave Hawk, Soaring Eagle and several other warriors wasted no time leaving the village as the trip to Fort Strother would take two suns. The group felt the need to get back on the Tallapoosa as soon as possible.

"My mother, I do not feel good in my heart about this decision to talk with this man called Jackson. He is not to be trusted." Little Flower said to Sunflower Woman as the two women prepared the evening meal for the twins.

"I too think he is not to be trusted." Sunflower Woman said, not showing the fear she felt. "Our micco, Brave Hawk and Soaring Eagle are intelligent men and good leaders. They will do what they think is best for our people."

"I know this, mother. I am still so afraid and I feel that bad, terrible things will happen soon to us," Little Flower said as she heard the voice of her daughter.

"Mother, mother," Little Deer called out. "Why can I not go too?"

"Go where, my daughter," Little Flower asked her excited child.

"With my father, I want to see Sharp Knife Jackson. I want to tell him to leave us along or I will, I will shoot him in his eye with my bow and arrow," the brave little girl said.

"I do not think that it will be necessary for you to go, Little Deer. Where is your brother?"

"Oh, he has left to follow our father," Little Deer said.

"What? When? How long ago," Little Flower said, almost screaming at the child.

"Just a little while ago, he said he would bust my nose if I told. I am not afraid of him. He will be the one with the nose that shows of blood."

"My mother, stay here with this child that is much too brave for her own good!" Little Flower said as she raced out of the huti.

"The sun will soon set my daughter. Take someone with

you. Please use care," Sunflower Woman said, holding her granddaughter back as the little girl attempted to follow her mother.

Fortunately, Little Deer had no fear of her brother and their mother was able to catch up with him before he had gotten too far from the village. Seeing him ahead on the path just as the shadows began to fall, Little Flower called out to her son. "Red Fox, stop now. Where do you think you are going?"

"She told. She will have a nose covered with blood for this," the disappointed little boy said. "If I had just a little longer, you would not have caught up with me."

Turning her son to look at her, Little Flower said, "Little Deer will not get a nose of blood and you are very fortunate she told me. What do you mean by doing this?" Do you not understand how serious this trip is and how dangerous? This could have caused your father and the others much trouble and someone could have …" she paused to catch her breath, realized how scared she was, "you could have been hurt."

"My mother, I am sorry to cause you to be afraid. I just wanted to go and see this man who comes to our land with no fear and kills our people. I just wanted to ask him to please leave us alone and go back to where he came from. We have done nothing to hurt him. Oh, mother, I am so afraid. I know this bad man will kill us. Oh, my mother," the little boy fell into the arms of his mother, tears running down his brown face, a face his mother knew might never become that of a man. The two walked hand and hand back to the village. Nothing else was said about a nose that showed of blood.

Chapter Twenty-Three

The Hillabee micco and his entourage made better time than expected on their trip up the Coosa. The group had been surprised at the number of soldiers camped near Fort Strother. Never before had they seen as many men in one place, the veteran soldier dressed in military blue, the raw-boned settler clad in home spun and the friendly Creek, who were camped near the edge of the vast compound, dressed in a combination of Creek and white clothing.

Robert Grierson led the group cautiously into the encampment. He had sent a runner ahead to ask and receive permission to enter with his group of Hillabee warriors. Permission had been granted just as the first request had been to come and speak with Andrew Jackson.

The Hillabee walked single file into the camp, their faces not showing any sign of the fear they felt. All of them were aware of the position they were in. They had just entered the camp of the enemy and each soldier stood with his long rifle ready to be fired upon command, if ordered to do so.

"I am Robert Grierson, trader of Hillabee town." Grierson said slowly, hoping to conceal his discomfort. What if he had brought his friends into a death trap? All of them could be shot instantly. "We have received permission from General Andrew Jackson to come here and ask for peace. These men are the micco from Hillabee."

A youthful looking man with insignia on his jacket that indicated his rank as a sergeant stepped forward. The sneer on his face showed his contempt for Grierson and the Hillabee. "All weapons must be removed and placed before the fire. When this is done, I will see if the General wishes to speak with you."

At this command, the delegation of Hillabee began moving back, only stopping when Grierson spoke softly, and telling them to obey the order. Small beads of perspiration began to show on his face as he laid his musket down and asked the Hillabee to do the same.

Refusing to part with the knives concealed under their belts, the Hillabee warriors placed their bows by the gun. The arrogant sergeant then turned and entered one of the canvass tents that lined the center of the camp. Only a short time had passed before Andrew Jackson followed by a beady-eyed man exited the tent.

"General Jackson, sir," the sergeant said, suddenly changing his demeanor to one of respect. "These Indians and this trader are from a town called Hill, Hill be. They would like to talk with you, sir, if you have the time and will hear them."

"Thank you sergeant, yes, I will listen to them." Jackson said turning to face the Hillabee warriors. "Please sit down." Robert Grierson sat down, the Hillabee remained standing, their dark faces showing no emotion as they sized up the man called Sharp Knife Jackson. They were not impressed by the man, his reddish hair in disarray, his clothing crumpled and wrinkled. His watery blue eyes had the slight look of that of a crazed man as he looked at each of the Hillabee warriors.
"I am General Andrew Jackson from the Army of the West Tennessee Volunteers and this is Major John Coffee. The government of the United States of America has sent us here to quell the uprising of the Creek Nation. You have brought this on yourselves by the brutal massacre of the white women and children at Fort Mims in the Tensaw Territory. We do intend to fulfill the job we have been sent to do. What do you of the Hillabee have to say?"

The Hillabee warriors, understanding what had been said remained silent. Trader Grierson would be their spokesperson. "General Jackson, sir, I am Robert Grierson and I have been the only trader at the town of Hillabee on the Tallapoosa for more than twenty-five years. These men and their families are my friends. They are good people and they have never been anywhere near the Tensaw area. They are not responsible for what occurred there. Most of them have tried to remain neutral during this period of unrest between the Creek and the white man and even between their Red Stick brothers. They wish no harm to the white people and only want to live in peace." Robert Grierson quickly said, realizing he would not be allowed much time to speak.

"Mr. Grierson," Jackson said, pulling his sword from the scabbard at his waist.

"There are many Creek in the Coosa and Tallapoosa River valleys that had nothing to do with the Mims Massacre." He slowly ran his gloved fingers over the sharp edge of the sword, making Grierson's skin tingle. "And these very people are even now making plans of attack. Why do you expect me to think the Hillabee will be any different?"

"Sir, I will swear on the Holy Bible if you wish. The Hillabe people will not fight against you. Please, just leave them alone. Do them no harm," Robert Grierson said, silently praying that this crazed man bent on destroying the Creek people would allow his Hillabee family to live.

"So be it Mr. Grierson. Take your Hillabee friends back to the Tallapoosa. I will do them no harm, but if I hear they plan attacks on me or my men," Jackson paused, looking at the Hillabee with a burning hatred, "I will make them pay. Good day, sir."

With an obvious dismissal, Grierson and the Hillabee warriors retrieved their weapons and left the enemy camp. They realized the danger was still present and while not running, no time was wasted in putting distance between them and the glaring soldiers, some even seemed disappointed that the order was not given to fire on the Hillabee.

The Hillabee micco gave the sign for silence and the group followed the path back down the Coosa, only stopping to rest when they reached the path which turned toward the rising sun and the Tallapoosa. Two warriors had slowed their pace and watched the path, making sure they had not been followed by any of the trigger-happy soldiers. As the two reached the other Hillabee, a time of rest was called by the micco.

"Is the path clear," The micco asked. "Are we being followed?"

"No one is following us," one answered.

"Then we will rest for a short while and eat some dried corn. We will not sleep until we return to our town. My brothers, I do not trust Sharp Knife Jackson or any of his men. He said he will do us no harm. He does not speak the truth. He is like the serpent and will strike when we least expect it. Robert Grierson, what opinion do you have of Jackson," the micco asked the man who had been his friend for more years than he could remember.

After a long silence, Grierson answered. "I too do not trust him. He is filled with an unnatural hatred for the Creek people and I believe he meant what he said. If the Hillabee people take up arms against him, he will kill you, all of you. We did all we could do to prevent this from happening and I pray to the Great Spirit that he will at least be a man of his word," Grierson said, his voice breaking.

The group walked until they reached the safety of their Tallapoosa home with the sounds of many owls echoing around them.

Chapter Twenty-four

One-hundred miles to the north, General John Cocke with the East Tennessee Volunteers was upset. He was still stewing over the fact that Andrew Jackson had been selected as the commander to put down the uprising of the Creek in the southern frontier. The two men were not friends, one always being jealous of the other. Wanting to best Jackson, Cocke had commanded one of his officers, General James White, to go deep into Creek territory. The orders included burning several villages, taking captives and killing any who resisted. One of the villages on the list was the Hillabee mother town. Cocke did not know, or did not care about the peace arrangement made between the Hillabee and General Jackson ...

The moon was high in the night sky when the fatigued Hillabee micco and his warriors returned home. Each went directly to his huti. The micco would inform the town people of the words of Jackson before the sun was high the following day. Soaring Eagle quietly slid under the blanket beside Little Flower, hoping not to wake her.

"My Eagle, I am so glad you are home. I feared for your safety," Little Flower said, wrapping her arms around her husband. "Please tell me the Hillabee people will escape the wrath of the white soldiers."

Soaring Eagle returned the embrace of his wife and held her close before speaking. "My Little Flower, my sweet flower. I do not know. Trader Grierson talked for us. He said that we, the Hillabee, only want peace and that we will surrender to Jackson if he will let us live. Oh, my flower, this man Jackson has the look of evil about him. He has a great hate for all red people. He said we can live if we do not fight against him or his soldiers." Soaring Eagle stopped speaking, pulling his wife closer to him. "If we do not do as he has said, we will die, all of us."

Little Flower caught her breath. "Then we will not fight and we will live," she said as tears began to fall.

"Little Flower, I do not trust him," Soaring Eagle added. "I have great fear of this man. I do not think he will keep his word."

Shedding tears for their people, the Hillabee warrior and his wife listened to the mournful cry of the owl. Both now understood the meaning.

Chapter Twenty-five

Before the sun would rise for the third time, they came. Nearly one-thousand strong, volunteer infantry, the numerous cavalry units and three-hundred Cherokee warriors surrounded the Hillabee town. The shadows of night still covered the sleeping village. Just as the dark sky first began to turn a soft shade of gray, the barking dogs alerted the town people of the presence of intruders.

Many of the Hillabee people had been lulled into a sense of false security, thinking they would be safe. Seeing the mass of soldiers all around the village, some of them still did not understand their intentions and what was about to happen.

The group of Hillabee going out to greet the soldiers was the first to be fired on. They were all killed instantly. This included women. The village became a scene of horrific pandemonium. The thunderous sound of the large horses and musket fire filled the air, muffling the cries of anguish from the women and children, the men trying to protect their family. Those on the far side of the village bordering White Oak Creek had more time. "Flower, take the children and get Sun Flower Woman quickly, "Soaring Eagle shouted, pulling the twins from their couch. "Go up the path by the creek. Hide in the big rocks until it is safe. Then go to one of the other Hillabee villages. The soldiers will not come there."

"My Eagle," Little Flower began to say, but was interrupted by her husband.

"Go, Flower now! There is no time for talk," Soaring Eagle said, gathering his bow and pouch of arrows.

"But what of you," Little Flower cried.

Soaring Eagle pulled his wife to him for only a brief moment. "If it is the will of the Giver of Breath, I will be with you soon. I must help defend our people now. Go!" He yelled as he left the huti in the direction of the musket fire and screams.

Little Flower did as she was told, pushing the terrified children ahead of her. Sunflower Woman was coming out of her huti with a blanket filled with items needed for survival. "My daughter, let us hurry, they will be here very soon."

"My father, where is he," Little Flower asked, wondering if she would ever again see her husband and her father.

"He is with Soaring Eagle and Brave Hawk and all of the other men of the Hillabee. Hurry, Little Flower, the soldiers are coming closer. Children run as fast as you can to the path by the creek," Sunflower Woman said, using her wisdom and strength to take control, fearing that her daughter could not.

Once on the creek path, Sunflower Woman realized that other women and children had been told to flee for their lives as well. Many were crossing the creek and going to what remained of the farm of Trader Grierson. She and Little Flower would go to the rocks to hide and wait.

The soldiers continued to overrun the Creek town, seeming to search for the Red Stick warriors that were grouped together. Others in their path met with the same fate. The soldiers fired their muskets and brandished their swords on the rush of Creek men who had tried in vain to make a stand of defense. The village square was quickly covered with dead or dying Hillabee warriors. The other warriors, realizing their only recourse, began to take cover and slip into the woods.

It was over. The Hillabee town who had asked for peace had received their answer. The town had been torched. Only a few huti remained standing. Sixty warriors had been killed and two-hundred sixty Hillabee people had been captured and forced to go with the soldiers, their destination unknown to them. General White was later heard to say that he had wiped out an entire village and that his men had not lost one drop of blood. He did not say that his soldiers had laughed as they murdered helpless Hillabee women and children, just as they had when they slaughtered their husbands and fathers.

Chapter Twenty-six

Sunflower Woman and Little Flower along with the children hid deep within the cave-like shelter of the large rocks that bordered the little creek. They could hear the musket fire and the cries of the women who had not had time to hide. They could smell the smoke from the burning village. They knew what had happened. Both women silently cried, knowing the loss of life was likely great and fearing for their men. The children, old enough to understand the danger, sat in silence, their small bodies trembling in fear.

Long after the sound of attack had diminished and the sunlight filtered through the cracks in the rocks, the women and children remained in their safe place, thinking it best to remain there rather than try to escape to one of the other Hillabee villages. Sunflower Woman heard footsteps on the dry leaves in the path. She quickly pulled her family away from the small opening, hoping to avoid being seen. Holding their breath, the sound of steps faded away and then was heard returning. Sunflower Woman moved slightly, allowing herself to see. She saw the brown legs of a warrior. Fearing the warrior was a part of the attacking group who would do them harm, she remained silent. Suddenly, a familiar voice quietly called out, "Little Flower, Sunflower Woman."

Recognizing the voice, Little Flower quickly slid from between the rocks, followed by her mother and children. "My Eagle, my ..." Seeing the blood streaming from the arm of her husband, Little Flower stopped. "You are badly wounded. Tearing a strip of cloth from her skirt, she quickly wrapped his arm, stopping the flow of blood. She gingerly touched the large lump on his head.

Soaring Eagle grimaced and pulled back, "I am not badly injured. The soldiers have left. We must go back and help ... the," he stopped, choking back a sob, "others. Oh, my Flower. So many of our people have been killed and injured and we have no village."

Sunflower Woman in a tone of strength, softly asked, "What of my husband and my son? Do they live or," she could not bring herself to finish her words.

"Sunflower Woman, I do not know. Many, like me, were left for dead, but live. Many others were taken captives and were forced to go with the soldiers." Soaring Eagle looked at his trembling children, tears sliding down their cheeks. "Red Fox and Little Deer, I want you to be brave and stay here in the rocks. We must return to what is left of our village. There are many who need our help. Do not leave until one of us comes back for you." He smiled at the twins. "Understand?"

"Yes, my father, we understand," Red Fox answered.

"I want to go help," Little Deer said.

"You can help later," Sunflower Woman said to her granddaughter. "Go back inside the rocks for now. Open the blanket. There is food. Do as your father asked and do not be afraid."

"Yes, grandmother," both children said as they crawled back inside the rock cave.

Chapter Twenty-seven

Soaring Eagle, his wife and the mother of his wife, hurried back to what had been the village. Others were beginning to come out from the places of hiding. Sunflower Woman was happy to see the wife and children of Brave Hawk coming from the Grierson Farm. "The farm house was not burned?" She asked Soaring Eagle.

"No, the white soldiers started to cross the creek but were stopped by their leader. That is good. Many of the women and children were safe there," Soaring Eagle said as they reached the edge of what was once a thriving Hillabee village.

All three stood in silence, the women not believing what they saw. The smoldering huti, the mass of dead and wounded Hillabee men, women and even children, loud cries from the injured and the keening from the surviving women filled the air with a sound of sorrow that had never before been heard in the Hillabee town. The owl circled over the square ground and then perched on the staff pole, the prophecy of death for many years being fulfilled.

Seeming to recover from her stunned shock, Sunflower Woman wiped the tears from her eyes and began to walk, "I need to find my husband and my son. I need to know if they still live."

Others began the search for family members, a search that lasted long into the day. The sound of keening or the cries of joy began afresh each time a loved one was found. Help for the forlorn Hillabee mother town soon arrived from one of the smaller satellite villages. The people from the Place to Find Fawns were equally shocked at the sights that laid before them. They wasted no time in separating the living from the dead. Those injured were immediately attended to and graves were dug for the others. Several mass graves contained entire families, the father, mother and their child. Food was given to any who could eat but few would eat.

As the sun began to sink in the western sky, the gruesome

duties of the day had been completed. Soaring Eagle stood and looked at the much diminished population of the Hillabee mother town. Many were gone, either dead or unaccounted for. He suddenly realized that he was the highest ranking micco still alive to serve in that position. The head micco had been severely wounded, the warrior who served as his second had been killed, as were two of the beloved men. Sunflower Woman had found her husband, barely alive. The determination of the two of them would see his improvement before the day was done. Brave Hawk, the best friend of Soaring Eagle and the brother of Little Flower was among those unaccounted for.

With a heavy heart, Soaring Eagle led the Hillabee people, the able and the wounded downstream to their new home, a Place to Find the Fawns. The Hillabee village that had been the home of their people for hundreds of years was now gone.

Chapter Twenty-eight

A time of great sadness and grief had settled over the Hillabee people. The family and friends at their new home tried to make them comfortable, providing food, clothing and building new huti for them. While this was greatly appreciated, spirits continued to be low and the Hillabee could not get past the devastation of their great loss.

The injuries of the micco had been severe and much time would be needed for his recovery. The remaining beloved men had then decided Soaring Eagle was the best suited to lead. Without the normal ceremony, Soaring Eagle was installed as head micco of all the Hillabee people, a position that in a different time would have been one of great honor for him. Now he accepted the position with trepidation, realizing the responsibilities of the Hillabee people were on his shoulders.

Later in the privacy of their new huti, Soaring Eagle confided in Little Flower, expressing his fear. "My wife, if these were happy times I would be joyful. I have had visions of being the micco of the Hillabee. My visions now are of more death and sorrow for my people. There is nothing I can do to prevent this. I fear, my Flower that I will prove to be an unfit micco."

"My Eagle, if the beloved men doubted your ability, another would have been chosen. Under these sad circumstances you will do as well as any warrior. No, you will do better. You love your people," Little Flower said, hoping to lift the mood of her husband. Still very sad herself, she did not tell her husband of her great fear for him. As he had said, there was much sorrow yet to come.

Chapter Twenty-nine

Soon after the attack on the Hillabee town, word came that the down-river town of Autossi had been attacked by soldiers from Georgia. They had suffered much the same fate, many being killed and the town burned. The world of the Creek had been shattered. No longer were they safe even in their own village.

Soon after hearing of the Autossi attack, a runner from Oakfuskee announced that Chief Menawa wished to address the Hillabee people. As they were gathering to hear the words of the great warrior chief, a commotion was heard coming from the edge of the village. Fearing the worst, the Hillabee began to scatter, the women seeking shelter and the men securing weapons. The women who saw what was taking place started their keening. This time the keening was a sign of joy instead of sorrow. As the crowd parted, six people, three men and two women, one carrying a child, came into view. With cries of joy, Spotted Fawn, Sunflower Woman and Little Flower ran to greet the group.

Brave Hawk first pulled his wife to him and then hugged his mother and sister. Family members of the others were equally excited. Soaring Eagle also ran to the side of his friend. The eyes of the two locked as they embraced. "My friend, it is with much happiness that I welcome you and the others back to our new home," Soaring Eagle said as the Hillabee gathered around. "Please, tell us where you were taken and how you managed to escape." Pausing, Soaring Eagle looked to his wife, "Little Flower, I think Brave Hawk and the others need food and water before they tell us about their experience."

Little Flower quickly did as her husband asked. The weary travelers sat down and ate for the first time since they had been taken captive, the women and the child silently shedding tears of relief.

The crowd of Hillabee people waited patiently until Brave Eagle indicated that he was ready to speak. As he rose, Soaring Eagle remembered the presence of Chief Menawa. "Brave Hawk, we are honored to have the great warrior Chief Menawa with us today." Looking in his direction, Soaring Eagle asked, "Chief Menawa, would you like to address our people before Brave Hawk speaks?"

With a strong voice, the big man replied, "I will talk after we hear of the experience of these brave people. Brave Hawk, please continue."

Brave Hawk stood and looked over the crowd of his Hillabee people, realizing that he did not see the faces of many of his friends. "My brothers and family, I am saddened to see so many missing. While I feel much sorrow for the lost of our Hillabee town, I am happy to see you who have survived the vicious attack by the white soldiers." He paused, taking a deep breath, "and the people of our own race from the north, the Cherokee." The Hillabee people listened in complete silence as Brave Hawk continued to relay the captive experience. "It seems that some Cherokee have sided with the white man and have joined with him in the fight against us. After the attack on our village, many of our people were forced by the soldiers to walk in the direction of the Cherokee homeland." He paused again, "their land joins that of the Creek and takes only three suns to reach the southern border. The white soldiers said the Cherokee could take the captives to have as slaves. Some of the Cherokee warriors agreed. Others said they did not want slaves; they would make us apart of their family. Just before we reached the Cherokee land, we stopped to drink water from a mountain stream. As we were drinking, a man without the look of the Cherokee tapped me on the shoulder. As I looked at him, he gave the signal of silence. He said to me, "I am of your people. Come with me." Not wanting to be shot in the back by the white soldiers, I hesitated. "Trust me, he said. Return to your ... to our people and tell them the Cherokee will not harm those taken captive. They will live as the Cherokee. Hurry, come." He stood in front of me, hiding me from the soldiers as they began to move again. I and the others," he pointed to the group beside him, "hid behind large boulders until the soldiers were out of our sight. We turned back on the path and did not stop until we reached …" Brave Hawk stopped again, "the remains of our town and saw only the fresh graves of our people."

Menawa stepped forward. "Thank you, my brother for this information. Did you hear talk of any plans for future attacks on the Creek people?"

"Yes, Brave Hawk said, "I overheard two soldiers dressed in the blue color of the army talking. One of them said that on our next trip down to this place, we will wipe out the rest of these savage people. The other soldier laughed and replied that he would like to take a pretty savage squaw home with him. If I could have gotten to him, I would have cut his throat," Brave Hawk said as the warriors around him began their war whoops.

Menawa nodded in agreement. "Thank you again, Brave Hawk." He turned to face the now much smaller Hillabee group, "My Hillabee people, I come here today to tell you of an important decision that has been made. The people of the Oakfuskee, the New Youka, the Eufaula, the Oakchay and the Fish Pond have decided to come together as one. We can not fight the soldiers as individual towns. With the strength of many, we can. I know the Hillabee have been lied to and deceived and now," the great warrior paused, a sadness filling his voice, "many of your people have been killed and many others taken from their home to a different place. I come to ask you to join us in our fight to keep our homeland and to preserve the very culture of the Muscogee people. Come with us down river to Cholocco Litabixee, the bend in the river that has the look of a flat shoe of a horse. There we will become many and strong. We will prepare to fight the soldiers and our own people and the Cherokee who choose to live as the white man. We will fight and we will defeat our foes or we will die making the Spirit of our grandfathers proud."

Menawa looked at the micco of the Hillabee as he stepped

aside. Soaring Eagle then looked at the three remaining beloved men and at Brave Hawk who now was second in the micco chain of power. "Do my people wish for us to talk of this or should a decision be made now?"

The oldest of the beloved men stood and spoke to Soaring Eagle softly, his voice raspy, his hand trembling as he placed it on the arm of the young micco. "Soaring Eagle, you are our leader now. If it is your decision for us to follow Menawa, then we will go and we will fight…to the end."

The others nodded in agreement. Soaring Eagle looked at the great warrior. "Chief Menawa, the people of the Hillabee are ready to follow the Oakfuskee to Cholocco Litabixee. We will meet the great enemy when they again come and we will not ever leave the home of the Muscogee."

Chapter Thirty

Preparations for the majority of the warriors to leave had not taken long. A few of them remained with the women, the children and the aged, who would make the trip when the town of the flat foot of the horse had been fortified and would be safe. Soaring Eagle made the trip down river and back many times between the season of cold and the season of new leaves. He felt a great responsibility for his people and wanted to know they were cared for. The father of Little Flower and the old micco were both still too weak from injuries received during the attack on the Hillabee town to make the trip. They realized they would need to heal so they could contribute later.

On a bitterly cold morning as he was preparing to go, Soaring Eagle noticed that his son was also packing his little pouch. "Red Fox are you planning a hunting trip on this cold morning," asked Soaring Eagle.

"No, my father, I am going with you. I have been practicing with my bow. My aim is good and I am ready to fight the soldiers," Red Fox said as he fastened the pouch to his belt.

Before Soaring Eagle could speak to his son, the voice of his daughter came from out of the darkness. "I am going too! I have a better aim. I can kill many white soldiers and I have food to take with us. Red Fox did not think of that," Little Deer said, proud that she had remembered the food.

Trying not to smile at the words of his children, Soaring Eagle quickly answered, "This is not the day for you to go." Realizing their disappointment he continued, "When I return all of our people will go and both of you will be by my side to lead the others. Now, since both of you are dressed for the cold, I think your mother needs rabbits for her stew. Do you think that each of you can bring one to her?"

"Yes, my father, I can," Red Fox said, his disappointment turning into joy.

"I can too, my father," Little Deer quickly added, "and mine will be the biggest."

That day turned into many and a full moon had passed before Soaring Eagle returned for his people. One final act needed to be done before the departure. Those who had lived in the destroyed mother town had gone back for one last look at the place that had been their home. Tears fell afresh as they viewed the burned huti and the fresh graves of their family and friends.

Sunflower Woman held tight to the arm of her injured husband as they stood in the spot where they had shared life for so many years. "We had a good life here. I am saddened to see this and it is with a broken heart that I leave," Sunflower Woman softly said as tears ran down her face. She turned to Brave Hunter, "Oh, my husband, I am not strong. I do not know if I can face tomorrow and the days after. What will happen to us now, to our children and to their children? What is to prevent the white soldiers from coming to the place of the flat foot of the horse and doing the…" She waved her arm around the burned village, "same there?"

"Sunflower Woman, my beautiful wife, you are my strength and our children look to you for their strength. My wife, we need for you to carry on. You must continue to be strong. I do not know what will happen. I cannot make promises for the days ahead," Brave Hunter said, pulling his wife close with his good arm. "We all must be strong."

"My mother," Little Flower called. "Soaring Eagle said it is time for us to go." She had watched her mother and father, not wanting to interrupt the private moment.

"Yes, my child, it is time to go. All that remain here are memories and the spirit of our people. And that spirit will go with us wherever we may go." Sunflower Woman said, feeling renewed strength as she wiped the tears from her sad eyes. Taking the hand of her Little Flower, she began to walk toward the husband of her daughter, the micco of the Hillabee.

Soaring Eagle watched as the small group of people, all that now remained of the once large village, gathered around him. "My people," Soaring Eagle looked at each man and each woman. "I can do nothing to change what has happened to us. I can do nothing to change what may happen in the future. I want each of you to know that I would have given my life to have prevented this," he waved his hand around the desolate village, just as Sunflower Woman had done. "I will lead you and all of the other Hillabee people to the best of my ability. The Hillabee are strong as are all of the Creek. We will persevere and we will give thanks to the Great Spirit for each new day. Let us go now. The other towns of the Hillabee will join us and we will all make our way by the waters of the magnificent Tallapoosa to our new home. People from the other towns that Chief Menawa told us of will already be there. The warriors have worked to make this a safe place. The white soldiers and the Creek and Cherokee who are friendly to them will again come. Soon they will try to kill us or take us away to a different land. We will fight and when the battles are over, the Hillabee people will still stand and we will return to the home of our grandfathers. Come, we have many miles to cover before we reach the Flat Foot of the Horse, which will now be called Tohopeka, the Village within the Fort." Soaring Eagle finished speaking to the small band of Hillabee with a new sense of strength, just as Sunflower Woman had. They had been told for many seasons to be ready; the time would come when they would need to fight. They were now ready.

Part Four
Tohopeka
Time of the New Leaves
1814

Chapter One

The number of Hillabee once again became great as the people of the four smaller towns and the remnants of the mother town fell in behind Soaring Eagle. Just as he had promised, his son and daughter were at his side. Little Flower and her mother and father followed, helping to support the old micco as he walked. The group, including the children, was somber and quiet as they began the trip. All of them realizing and fearing the danger of what lie ahead.

The bright sunshine of the day before had given way to heavy clouds; the wind blew cold, causing some of the older women to pull their blankets closer. The path from the Hillabee towns was lined with the dark pink flower of the redbud tree, the blooms providing the only brightness on the otherwise dreary day. The Hillabee people continued on at a brisk pace, as Soaring Eagle hoped to reach Tohopeka before darkness fell. Just as the Hillabee reached the wider path that led to the town, the now familiar sound of the owl began its mournful cry. The group stopped, looking from one to another, remembering the omen of what the owl represented. One of the women from the mother town who had lost her husband began to cry out, "I cannot go any further. I cannot face any more death and sorrow."

Another woman began to keen, others following her lead. Feeling a moment of panic, Soaring Eagle looked back at the group. "My people, please do not stop. We must reach Tohopeka while there is light. We can not be on the trail when darkness falls," he admonished. He did not tell them his scouts had seen signs of soldiers nearby. "We do not have too much farther to go. Please start moving again," Soaring Eagle pleaded.

One of the beloved men moved forward parting the women. "People of the Hillabee, we must listen to our new micco. He is our leader now. We must go," he spoke, using the wisdom of his many years. With that the Hillabee people began moving, walking faster than before.

Chapter Two

The tired, nervous Hillabee group reached Tohopeka shortly before nightfall. Being the last of the towns to arrive, they would be near the river. The women of the other towns quickly helped the late arrivals to make camp before darkness covered the town. After making sure his people were safely settled, Soaring Eagle left to be with the other miccos and warriors in the make-shift square ground. He could hear the war chants of the prophets as they incited the already enthusiastic men. As he entered the square, the chants subsided and the micco Menawa stood. He looked at Soaring Eagle, obviously glad to see him.

"Soaring Eagle, are the women and children of the Hillabee settled? Do they have food," Menawa asked as quietness settled over the group.

"Yes, Menawa, my people are comfortable," Soaring Eagle said, surprised to be singled out by the chief.

"Good, we have important words to say. Monahee of the Okfuskee will serve as head micco during the upcoming days. He will now talk of our plan of action," Menawa said as he took his place beside Soaring Eagle and the other micco.

"My people," Monahee said in a loud imposing voice. "We have all gathered here in the great bend of the Tallapoosa for one reason. As you are aware, the white soldiers under the leadership of Sharp Knife Andrew Jackson, along with his friendly Creek and Cherokee, are again coming to do battle with us. My scouts say they are only two suns away and their numbers are great." Monahee paused as many warriors gave loud war whoops while others looked surprised at how close the upcoming encounter appeared. "We have worked to build this strong barricade," he pointed in the direction of the vast log structure that extended across the neck of land enclosed by the river. "It is strong and we will be protected from the bullets of the white soldiers when they come. The time of the battle may be long and …" he paused again, "and as it is in all battles, some of our warriors will not live. For the safety of our women and children, any who wish to go will be taken down river to Elkahatchee Creek. We now will prepare ourselves for the battle that will come."

The chants of the prophets began again. The near naked men, their bodies painted black and red, danced around and around the fire, their war chants becoming louder. The Red Stick warriors, their numbers reaching over one-thousand, quickly responded and joined with the prophets. The deafening noise of the war whoops covered the now melancholy sound of the owl.

Chapter Three

Andrew Jackson and his force had camped at Fort Williams on the Coosa River, just over fifty miles from the horseshoe. He knew about the large group of Red Sticks waiting for him on the Tallapoosa. He also knew they had built an extensive fortification which he planned to obliterate.

His men were seasoned and ready to fight. They had been through difficult times, not having adequate food supplies, no pay and being far from home, their enlistment term being nearly over causing some insubordination. Many of them had told General Jackson they were going home. A remark the feisty General would not tolerate. The men were told they would stay and that they would fight or they would suffer the consequences. Understanding what the no-nonsense leader implied, the group became very efficient and ready to fight this bunch of Indians that had created so much trouble.

Just days before the Hillabee group left the sad remains of their mother town, General Jackson and his soldiers, the Tennessee Volunteers and the friendly Creek and Cherokee, began their march south. Blazing a trail through the heavily wooded area, the large contingent of fighting men, over 3,000 strong, made camp five miles from Tohopeka. The following day would be one of destiny for the Creek Nation.

Chapter Four

The day according to the calendar of the white man was Sunday, the 27th day of March in the year 1814. The morning dawned clear and cool. Monahee called his micco and warriors together for one last talk before final preparations began. He stood and looked out at the one-thousand painted warriors, most of all the warriors who remained on the northern Tallapoosa.

"My warriors, my brave Creek brothers, my scouts tell me the white soldiers are on the move from Emuckfau Creek where they have camped. Before the sun is overhead, the battle will have begun. We will be out-numbered. My scouts say by as many as three to one. They will have two of the big guns that are pulled by horses," Monahee paused, waiting for this information to be understood before he continued; "The odds are against us. My brothers, do not be discouraged. We are Creek warriors. The Great Spirit will be with us here on this spot where we have gathered to defend our home and our people. We have constructed this great barricade. The bullets of the white man cannot break through." He paused, his tone changing, "If we are overwhelmed, some can retreat to the river where our women wait. Canoes have been placed on the bank. Our women and children can be taken to the other side to escape the bullets of the white soldiers. Go now and prepare for the battle that will soon be." Monahee then stepped aside as Menawa walked forward.

"My brothers, I would like to have one final word. We are warriors of the mighty Creek Nation. We are brave and strong. On this day, we will be pushed no farther. We will make a stand here on the banks of the Tallapoosa, the home of our grandfathers and the fathers of their fathers. We will fight as long as we have breath to fight. We will live or…, we will die the honorable death of the Creek warrior." As Menawa finished, one-thousand red war clubs were brandished in the air and the voices of the Red Stick warriors echoed across Tohopeka.

The warriors returned to their women and children before final preparations for the battle were made. Soaring Eagle and Brave Hawk walked to the camp of their family, both realizing this could be for the last time. Red Fox and Little Deer ran to their father and climbed into his outstretched arms. "My brave son and daughter, the time has come for me and the other warriors to fight for you and our people. Promise me you will continue to be brave and help your mother," Soaring Eagle said, pulling his children close. "Do not ever forget that you are of the mighty Creek Nation."

"My father, we are ready to fight too," Red Fox said as he bravely pulled his bow from his shoulder.

"Yes, I have many arrows in my bag. I will hurt many white soldiers if they come near me," Little Deer said, trying to hold back the tears that threatened to fall from her huge brown eyes.

Soaring Eagle, feeling the urge to cry as well, smiled again at his children. "If the white soldiers come close, fill them full of arrows and keep them away from your mother." He turned to look at his waiting wife; her tears could not be held back and were falling freely down her beautiful face. "My Little Flower, my Flower," he said, tenderly brushing the tears from her cheek. "My love for you is more than all the stars in the sky." Just as he was about to continue with his farewell endearments, the sound of drums were heard coming from the area of the barricade. This was a signal that the army of Jackson had been sighted and was near Tohopeka. Soaring Eagle knew it would take time to return to the log breastwork, located a good distance from the village. He and the other warriors would need to go immediately. He pulled his wife close, holding her tight. "Be brave, my Flower." He turned to Sunflower Woman who was still clinging to her husband. "Take care of Little Flower and the children. Come Brave Hunter, Brave Hawk, It is time."

Chapter Five

General Andrew Jackson checked his pocket watch… 10 o'clock. He had divided his large group of soldiers, sending his much respected friend John Coffee with his Tennessee Volunteers and the friendly Indians ahead to cross the river. If the hostiles were encircled they would not be able to escape. His plan was total annihilation of the Red Stick warriors. When he topped the hill, Jackson was amazed at what he saw in front of him. The hostiles had constructed a vast double barricade made from timber that was higher in height than any of the soldiers. The pine log structure was constructed with strategic firing holes for defense and it extended entirely across the peninsula. "Quite a piece of work for these people to accomplish," he said, "But they have created a trap for themselves, making escape impossible."

By 10:30 that morning, the cannons were in place and Jackson began firing on the barricade. The balls flying through the air came just short of the target or inflicted little damage to the log barricade, doing no harm to the painted warriors inside. The war whoops and chants coming from the Red Sticks were deafening. The prophets ran from end to end of the log structure, encouraging the warriors. Some had flintlock muskets and ammunition; these would need to be saved for later when the soldiers came closer. An occasional arrow soared through the air, mostly as a show of defiance. The arrows too would need to be saved. The Red Sticks knew Sharp Knife Jackson had not come to play games and this was just a precursor of what was to come.

Chapter Six

General John Coffee with his men and friendly Creek and Cherokee had crossed the swiftly moving river. They were positioned across from the village and were concealed just out of view. They waited impatiently. They could hear the blast of the cannon fire and the war whoops of the Red Sticks. Still they waited and watched the movements of the women and children. The sun was now high in the sky. Was this wait to continue or was a battle to be fought on this day? Unable to wait any longer, several Cherokee warriors had moved close enough to see the canoes on the other side of the river. Without orders or permission from the commanding officer, they slid into the cold, swift river and swam to the other side…

Sunflower Woman and Little Flower tried in vain to remain calm. They too heard the sounds coming from the hill near the barricade and they realized the real battle had not yet begun.

"My mother," Little Flower asked, with fear in her voice. "Do you think our warriors will win this battle? Do our people have a chance to survive?"

Sunflower Woman looked at her daughter as another blast from the big gun filled the air. "My daughter, my child, I have always spoke the truth to you. I have taught you to be strong. You will need that strength now. Many of our warriors will not live to see the sun set on this day. I do not know what will happen to us."

"My mother," the small voice of Little Deer was barely heard over the den of noise. "I need a drink of water. Can I please go to the spring to get some? The water jar is empty. Red Fox will go with me."

Not aware of the soldiers waiting on the other side or the Cherokee who had swam the river; Little Flower reluctantly gave her daughter permission to go. "We do need water, go quickly there and come right back," She said. "We should stay close together."

"Do not go near the river, Little Deer," Sunflower Woman said, "and be quick."

Little Deer and Red Fox quickly picked up the water bottles and ran in the direction of the spring-fed branch that emptied into the river. Hearing a splash, both children stopped. "Did you hear that Red Fox," Little Deer whispered to her brother.

"Yes, and the sound came from the river," Red Fox answered.

"I am going to see what it was," said Little Deer.

"Our grandmother said for us not to go to the river," Red Fox warned.

Paying no attention to her cautious brother, Little Deer began walking the short distance to the river, slowly parting the bushes that lined the bank. "Red Fox, come quickly," She whispered. "Look," Little Deer pointed at three warriors with white feathers in their hair swimming across the river.

"Who are they," Red Fox asked.

"They are our enemy. Run tell our mother," Little Deer exclaimed.

"Are you not coming with me," Red Fox asked with obvious fear for his sister.

"I will watch to see what they will do, hurry," Little Deer insisted, pushing her brother toward the village.

The little girl watched as the warriors swam the cold river. She looked across and saw the movement of many on the other side. The warriors climbed out of the water, not seeing the child in the bushes. Touching the pouch of arrows hanging from her shoulder, the child remembered that she had promised her father she would shoot the soldiers and this warrior obviously came to fight with them. Little Deer slowly notched the arrow and pulled tightly. Just as the lead warrior stepped clearly into her view, Little Deer released her arrow. Having spent much time in competition with her brother, her aim was true, hitting the Cherokee squarely in the stomach. Not having the strength to cause deep penetration, Little Deer's shot resulted in little pain but great surprise. The Cherokee could hear the sounds of the battle and the noise from the village, but he saw no one. Where did the arrow come from?

Little Deer smiled when she realized she had hit her target. She slowly stepped back from the bush, holding her breath, fearing any movement would give away her hiding place. She could still see the warriors, her victim pulling the arrow from his stomach, the blood showing through his white hunting shirt. He indicated to the others that he was not badly injured and the group went about their mission. They quickly slid three large canoes into the river.

Red Fox ran back to the village as fast as he could. "My mother, my mother," he shouted as he came in sight of Little Flower.

Hearing the fear in her son's voice, Little Flower ran to meet him. Seeing that Little Deer was not with him, a feeling of dread washed over her. "Your sister, Red Fox, where is she?"

"My mother, she is not hurt. She is hiding and watching the warriors swim the river," Red Fox said as Sunflower Woman rushed to his side.

"Warriors, do you know who they are and where they came from," Sunflower Woman questioned.

"I do not think they are Creek and they have white feathers in their hair. They were swimming all the way across the river," Red Fox said breathlessly. "I think I should go back and get Little Deer. They may hurt her," Red Fox exclaimed as he turned to go, suddenly feeling responsible for his sister.

"No, you will stay here," Little Flower said. "I will get your sister. My mother, go and tell the others that White Stick warriors that we knew were coming are entering the village from the river. We will need to try and stop them. If they come, we will be trapped."

Chapter Seven

Little Deer watched wide-eyed as the trio hurriedly made their way back to the other side of the river. In only minutes the canoes were filled with other Cherokee and Creek making their way back. By the time she realized that she should go back to the village the riverbank was filled with warriors wearing white feathers in their hair. Little Deer knew it was too late for her to escape. She must stay where she was.

Little Flower and two other women along with an old warrior who was not well enough to fight, moved quickly toward the river. They stopped abruptly as they heard the sound of the warriors shouting their plans to storm the village.

"Go quickly. Tell the women and all who are well enough to be ready. Send one of the boys who can run fast to the barricade to tell our warriors the White Sticks and soldiers are attacking us from the river. Hurry," Little Flower pleaded as tears welled in her eyes. "I must find my child."

She moved cautiously forward, staying concealed behind the bushes, daring not to call out for Little Deer. The warriors and some of the white soldiers who had crossed the river were beginning to make their advance toward the village. Little Flower knew her time of not being seen by the men was short. Then she saw her daughter only a few steps away, securely hidden by the new green leaves of a big bush. She placed a hand over her own mouth to avoid calling out for her. She watched as a tall, muscular brave, obviously a friendly Creek, walked very near the bush.

Seeing the warrior as well, Little Deer, thinking he would see her, decided she should run. At the precise moment she stepped from behind the bush, the warrior, hearing her movement, rushed to the other side, bumping into Little Deer and knocking her to the ground. Little Flower watched in horror as the two looked at each other. The warrior was surprised. The horrified child's scream could not be heard over the surrounding noise.

Looking around at the oncoming host of warriors and soldiers who had not yet spotted the child, he suddenly made the signal for silence. Turning again, making sure his action was not being watched, he picked up the frightened child and slid her back under the bush. The child thanked him with a timid smile. With that done, he joined the group of warriors heading toward the village, his white feather bobbing up and down as he walked.

Little Flower, not believing what she had witnessed, waited until the wave of men had gone past. Seeing that more were on the way, she crawled to the hiding place of Little Deer. She quietly slid under the bush with her child and whispered, "Oh my child, my brave child. We are in great danger now. Follow me. Move when I do. Stop when I stop. We have got to get back to Red Fox and my mother."

The two crawled underneath the cover of the bushes and reeds lining the river until they reached the small creek. Her intentions were to get back to the village quickly or they would be captured or killed. The strong-willed woman was determined to get back to her son and mother. She would not allow herself to think of her husband.

As Little Flower and Little Deer reached the village edge, the shouts and yells became louder. They could smell the smoke of new fires being lit around the huti. They watched the women and children, with muskets being pointed at them, pushed and shoved into a large circle away from the burning huti. Feeling a sharp object in her back, Little Flower realized they had been discovered. She and Little Deer were pushed into the group of keening women. She jumped as a firm hand grabbed her arm. "My daughter and my granddaughter, be still and show no resistance," Sunflower Woman said, holding the arm of Red Fox with her other hand. "I heard one of the soldiers say that we are not to be killed if we follow their orders."

The women stood and listened as the sound of the battle grew increasingly louder. The blasts of the cannons had stopped. The war cries grew louder. The women now realized the barricade had been breached and the prophecy of the owl had yet again been fulfilled.

Chapter Eight

For two hours General Andrew Jackson had fired his cannon and shot volleys of musket balls at the securely built barricade. He had sent his ready and willing men down the hill in an attempt to storm the log wall, each time calling them back as they were easy targets for the Red Stick warriors.

He had not given orders to Coffee, his volunteers nor the friendly Indians to attack the village from the rear; their mission was to prevent escape. Seeing the smoke from the burning village, he realized they had crossed the river and attacked. Taking advantage of the unanticipated action, Jackson immediately ordered his men to charge the barricade. Some of the Red Stick warriors had fallen back to the village, trying to protect the women and children.

The majority of the nearly one-thousand painted warriors prepared themselves as they watched three times as many adequately armed soldiers advance toward them. Several on the front line were killed as they neared the barricade and attempted to scale the wall. Once on the wall, Jackson's men were able to fire directly through the holes the warriors had fired from. For a brief period, musket touched musket. Then, the wall was breached and the stockade was filled with white soldiers.

On and on they fought, Jackson's men firing their muskets at close range and then using the bayonet to finish the work. The Red Stick warriors quickly used all of their ammunition and resorted to their weapons of old, the knife and bow and arrow. The ground was soon covered with the blood of the painted warriors. Monahee was among the first to go down, shot in the mouth as he screamed the war chant, encouraging his warriors to carry on. Menawa then became the valiant leader.

There was no place to go. No way to escape. The attacking soldiers from the village were ready and waiting to fire on any who tried to get to the river. The only choice was to fight and die, just as Creek warriors had been doing for generations. This is what would happen on this day. Soaring Eagle watched as one by one his friends went down. Then it happened. A great sadness filled his heart as the brother of his wife fell at his feet, a sword of a white soldier protruding from his stomach. The husband of Sunflower Woman had been sent back to protect the women and children. Soaring Eagle did not know he had been shot in the back while carrying a crying child to his mother. Soaring Eagle heard the sharp thug and instantly felt the pain from the butt of the musket being bashed on his head. He could now feel the warm blood running down his face. His last thought before he sank to the ground was that of his wife, his Little Flower.

Chapter Nine

The sounds of battle, the musket fire, the war cries and the cries of death continued on as the sun sank lower in the western sky. The women and children sat in silence, tears streaming down their brown faces as screams from their husbands, fathers and sons echoed along the river valley. The armed soldiers had encircled the group, ordering them to remain silent. The women watched in horror as an elderly, simple-minded man was struck in the head as he sat grinding corn, totally oblivious to what was happening around him. A red-faced, raw-boned man dressed in home-spun laughed as he retrieved his weapon, saying he wanted to tell the folks back home that he had killed an "injun."

Several of the women, including Sunflower Woman and Little Flower had been roughly shoved back into the circle as they tried to protect a small child. The hungry toddler had wandered from his mother's side and had asked a blue-clad soldier for food. The child was shot, killing him instantly. When the soldier was reprimanded for his action, he replied that the kid would have grown up to be a Red Stick.

The women had known of the slaughter that was happening near the barricade, even seeing some of the fighting as the warriors fell back behind piles of brush and trees. The women did not know of the tortured brutality their men had faced, even after they had breathed their last breath. They did not know the friendly Creek had scalped the felled warriors. Needing to have an accurate count of Red Stick dead, Sharp Knife Andrew Jackson had ordered his men to cut off the tip of their noses. The women did not know this, nor did they know that skin from the arms and legs of their husbands and sons had been stripped. The white soldiers wanted souvenirs and the tanned hide of these injuns would make a good belt or bridle.

The sounds of battle begin to diminish. Only the occasional shot fired at an already wounded warrior as he attempted to escape into the river was heard. Most of the nearly one-thousand Red Sticks lay in bloody heaps, lifeless and cold, the empty stare of the valiant warrior's eyes, never more to see.

Chapter Ten

The children, hungry and cold, began to cry. The women, led by Sunflower Woman, began their keening, loud and sorrowful. The soldiers guarding them looked from one to the other. One of them asked, "What are we to do with this bunch of crying children and what kind of racket are these women making?"

Another soldier answered, "General Jackson said they are to be taken captive. We are to move them all up river to the camp at Emuckfa Creek before nightfall. In the morning they will be divided. Some will be given to the Cherokee and some will be given to the friendly Creek who live on the Chattahoochee. William McIntosh, one of the leaders from a town called Coweta, will take many back with him. They can do with these squaws what ever they wish, make them into slaves or adopt them into their family. As for me, I will be happy for them to be the problem of someone else. We should get them moving now; it will be dark before we get to the camp."

With that the guards began to push the women and children forward toward the path that led up river. Not understanding, some resisted and were promptly struck down, others were hit with sticks like driven cattle. The children cried louder, the women forming lines of defense. Sunflower Woman stopped and turned to the guard nearest her. "Where are you taking us? Why are we being treated in this way," she asked, speaking English to the startled man.

"Well now, we have a squaw that can talk in something besides that injun jabble." A dirty faced man with stringy flaxen hair said, as he pushed Sunflower Woman to the ground. The action quickly brought several women rushing toward the man. "Get away from me you filthy bunch of heathens," the enraged soldier yelled as he pointed his musket at the women.

"Private," a neater looking soldier with yellow stripes on his sleeve said, stepping between him and the group of women, "Leave these people alone. Our orders are not to harm them unless absolutely necessary." He looked at Sunflower Woman, showing very little warmth. "We are taking you to our camp up river. In the morning you will be divided and taken to other places. For now you are our captives. I strongly advise you to do as you are told."

Sunflower Woman showed no fear as she again stepped forward. "We will do as we are told. Please, may we have a little time to prepare our hearts before we go? Let me have words with these people who are my Creek family."

The ranked soldier briskly nodded, "You may. Be ready when I tell you."

Sunflower Woman took the hand of Little Flower and turned to face the women and children along with a few old men who had also been taken hostage. "My family, my friends," She paused wiping the tears from her eyes. "On this day, the lives of Creek people have forever been changed. We no longer will live as we have in the past. We no longer have," choking back a sob, she continued, "our husbands, our sons, our fathers. We have dreaded this day for many seasons. We knew it would come. Prophesy has been fulfilled. The day of the owl has come, but now we must continue on. Our children must carry on with the spirit of the Creek people. This must never be allowed to perish. Let us do as we are told and we will live." Sunflower Woman and Little Flower, taking the hand of the each of the children, leading the over three-hundred captives, began walking in the direction the white soldier pointed. The strength of the two women would insure that the spirit of the Creek would continue to live for as long as the sun shall rise.

Chapter Eleven

Cool winds blew over the battlefield that was intended as a fortress for one-thousand brave Red Stick warriors. The fortress instead had become a trap of death. Only a fortunate few had survived. Menawa, injured repeatedly, lived. After being left for dead, he had concealed himself underneath the bodies of less fortunate warriors. When the opportunity allowed, he slipped into a canoe and floated under cover of darkness down the Tallapoosa River. Menawa would lead and fight again.

The warriors lying on the battlefield who had suffered the brutal execution by the white soldiers and their Indian allies would not live. This single battle had almost annihilated an entire nation of warriors. These warriors had fought bravely to the end, not asking for pardon. They had fought and died as their grandfathers would have expected them to do, as Creek warriors had done for generations.

As the last rays of the setting sun filtered over the mangled bodies of the brave warriors, the sad, mournful cry of the owl began. The cry that had been prophesies of death for the warrior was now the end of a way of life for the Creek people. A people who would survive that prophecy and the wrath of Andrew Jackson and others like him, a people who would regroup and rebuild and because of the eternal strength and spirit of the mighty Creek Nation, would live to see a new yet different day.

— The End —

Epilogue

While doing my research for *The Owl and the Horseshoe*, I was reminded of my first visit to Horseshoe Bend National Military Park. I was ten or twelve years old and my family had planned a trip to the park. I could barely contain my excitement as we first attended worship service at nearby Eagle Creek Baptist Church. It was very difficult for me to sit still and listen to the former pastor of our home church and even harder to mind my manners during lunch served at his home.

Finally, we could leave and go to the Horseshoe, the place I had read so much about. Having been established for only a few years, the park was not as spectacular as it is now. We toured the small museum. I was entranced, reading every word written about the artifacts and displays, my parents having to urge me on. We then took the slow ride around the battle ground. I remember standing by the fast moving Tallapoosa River, and turning to view the Tohopeka Village site, marked only with a plaque already defaced by an uncaring person. We moved on around the tiny road until we saw the reconstructed barricade, the stark row of logs stretching across the open meadow.

This was the place where so many painted warriors had tried in vain to defend their home. I recall the sadness that instantly filled me and I think that, even then, I knew I wanted someday to write about these people. Their story is one of the most tragic ever experienced by any race of people who called this country their home.

With the exception of Little Flower, Soaring Eagle and their families, all events in the book are true and historically accurate. I imagined myself there as I wrote and that I could hear the mournful call of the owl. Yes, the owl is also fictitious, but the Creek people actually were very superstitious and considered the screech owl an omen of misfortune. It well may have been that a family much like that of Little Flower and Soaring Eagle heard the melancholy cry of the owl. I hope my readers, too, were transported back to the Hillabee village and to Tohopeka as they read *The Owl and the Horseshoe*.

Glossary of Creek Words

Accee-Black drink

Chunkee-Game of chance played by Creek people using a round, smooth stone

Hinibas-Creek man responsible for planning celebrations

Huti-Creek house

Keening-High pitched cry produced by Creek women in time of sadness or joy

Keethla, Knower-Creek man with the power to predict the future

Micco-Creek Chief

Oakfuskee-Old name for Tallapoosa River and also a village site

Poskeeta-Busk or Green Corn Ceremony observed in late summer after first corn harvest

Sofkee-mush or soup made from corn

Town Cryer-Creek man who informs the village people of news and events

Acknowledgements

A Historical Analysis of the Creek Indian Hillabee Towns
Don C. East
(Used for research and historical accuracy)

Alabama Maps from Battle for the Southern Frontier
Mike Bunn and Clay Williams
& Struggle for the Gulf Borderlands
Frank Ousley, Jr.

Alabama Department of Archives and History

Photograph locations
Horseshoe Bend National Military Park
& Department of Transportation
Alabama Highway 22
Hillabee Creek Bridge

Front Cover Sketch of Tohopeka
Melessia Rothwein
(Author's Sister)

Editing Assistance
Harold "Pete" Cottle and Charles Pollard

And to my husband, Fred Randall Hughey for his
encouragement, support, patience, time and love.

Hillabee Creek was named for the Hillabee Village of Creek Indians. The mother village was located up the creek from the Alabama Highway 22 bridge where White Oak Creek enters the Hillabee.

Hillabee Creek Bridge on Alabama Highway 22 located between New Site and Alexander City, Alabama.

The Site of Tohopeka Village on the Grounds of Horseshoe Bend National Military Park.

White posts stretch out over the battleground at Horseshoe Bend National Military Park marking the approximate site of the Creek Red Stick barricade which extended across the neck of the "Horse's Flat Foot" or the Horseshoe Bend of the Tallapoosa River.

The Tallapoosa River at Horseshoe Bend. Creek and Cherokee who were friendly allies of General Andrew Jackson swam across at this site and took canoes from Tohopeka Village.

Horseshoe Bend National Military Park view of the north battlefield where white posts mark the approximate location of the Red Stick barricade. Hill at top left is near General Andrew Jackson's cannon position.

Map by Jessica McCarty.

The Owl and The Horseshoe

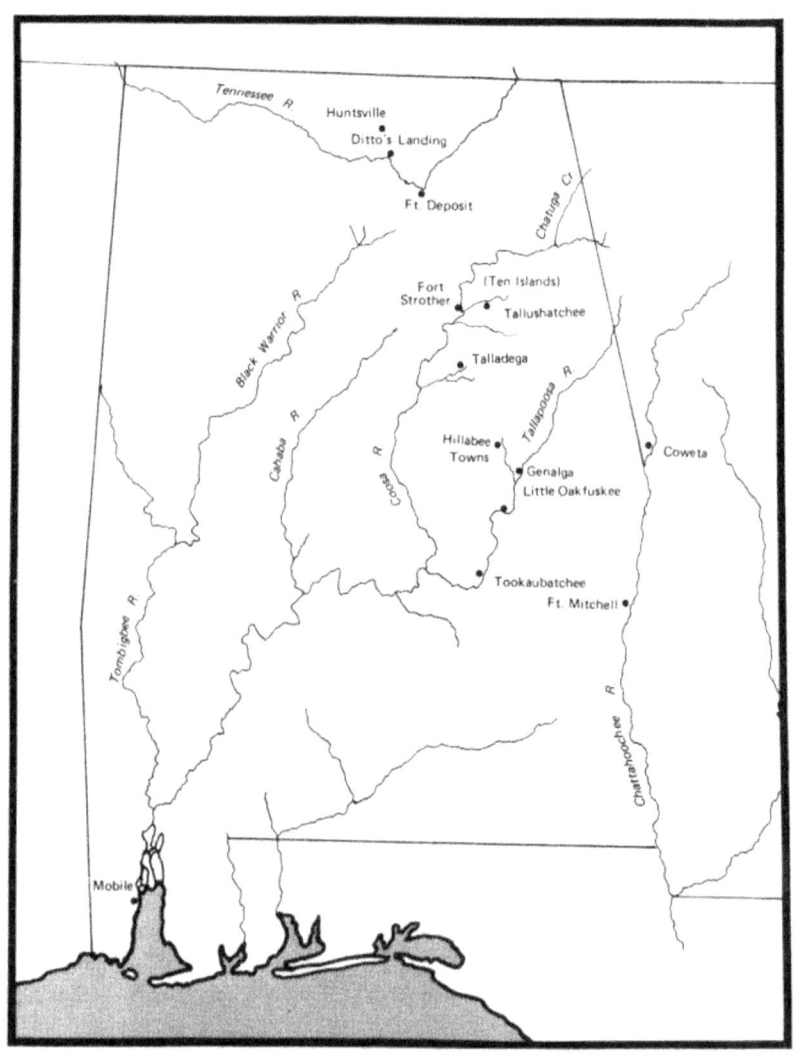

Creek Village Sites circa 1812.

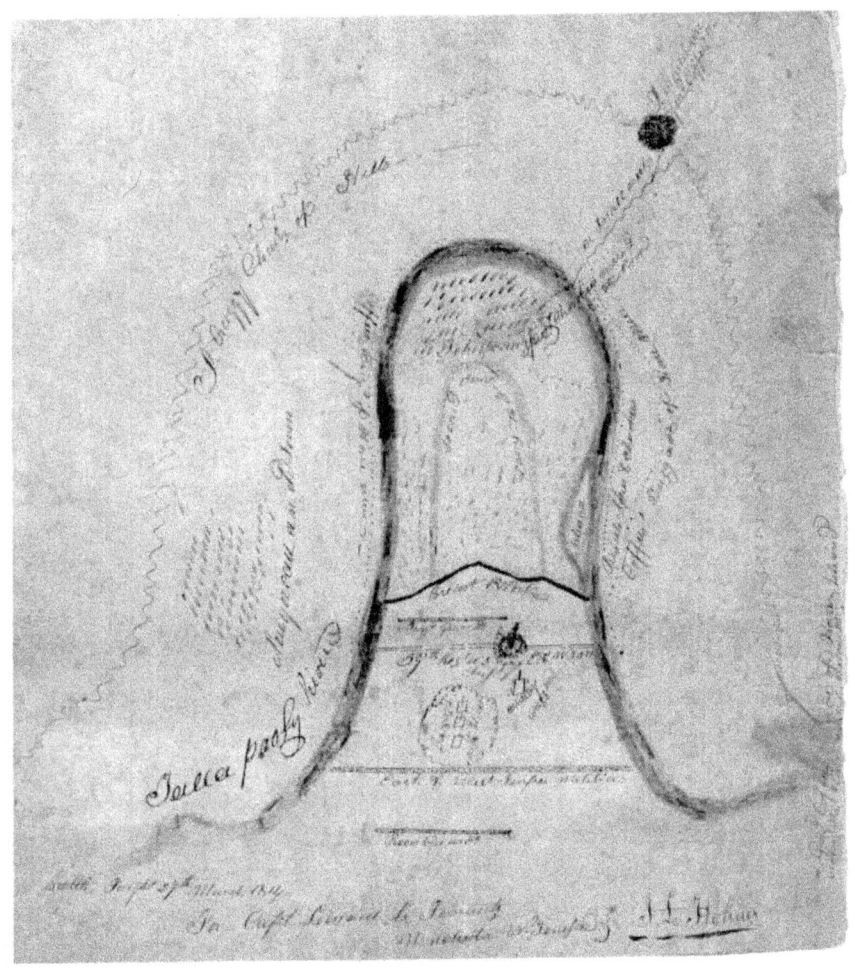

A map of the Battle of Horseshoe Bend, by Leonard Tarrant. *Courtesy of the Alabama Department of Archives and History.*

The Horse's Flat Foot or The Horseshoe Bend of the Tallapoosa River.

www.ingramcontent.com/pod-product-compliance
Lightning Source LLC
Chambersburg PA
CBHW071618080526
44588CB00010B/1174